Why Americans Have It All Wrong
An Alternative Way to Find Happiness—
Tales and Tips from a Corporate Lawyer Turned Expat Now
Semi-Retired Real Estate Investor

David Rosenfield

Buck the Trend Press—Denver, CO
ISBN: 979-8-218-50048-1
eBook ISBN: 979-8-3304-1078-1
Library of Congress Control Number: 2024918628
Title: *Why Americans Have It All Wrong: An Alternative Way to Find Happiness—Tales and Tips from a Corporate Lawyer Turned Expat Now Semi-Retired Real Estate Investor*
Author: David Rosenfield
Digital distribution | 2024
Paperback | 2024

Published in the United States by New Book Authors Publishing

Dedication

This is dedicated, with love and thanks, to my mom and stepdad. Particular thanks to my stepdad, to whom I owe a debt of gratitude for helping raise me from the age of 6, even as he did his part in raising his own three kids, the youngest of whom was 18 when he and my mother got married. Among my favorite memories growing up was playing "The Question Game." At dinner, my stepdad would question my sister and me about arithmetic, grammar, spelling and many subjects related to our grade level. He made it fun and I'm sure it has stuck with me as I developed a never-ending love of learning. And I will never overlook my mom, who is the most selfless person I will ever know. She is the type of person, who when going out to dinner with my stepdad when my sister and I were younger, would not only order something she knew I would enjoy, but then purposely not eat it all to be sure she would bring home leftovers home which she knew I would enjoy (even though she also provided our babysitter with money to order in). And this trend continued even when I lived with them for a couple of years after law school and during winter/summer breaks from college/law school.

I remain forever grateful and indebted to both of them. My stepdad had no legal or financial obligation to care for my sister and me (she's three years older than me), but did so just as he continued working well into his older years. As for my mother, considerably younger than my stepdad, I promised to always take care of her or see to it that she was in the "best home money could buy." In that regard, I recently bought a second home in Myrtle Beach, SC where she will (hopefully) visit/stay with me in her older years. So I hope you enjoy the book and spread the word/love to help contribute to that noble cause ☺.

Table of Contents

Introduction

In a recent study of twenty-one developed countries, the United States was the only country that didn't have a law guaranteeing its employees a minimum number of vacation days. In contrast, France *requires* its employees to take a minimum of thirty vacation days per year.

The United States is typically regarded as one of, if not the, greatest countries on Earth (or at least it was up until a few years ago before all its political turmoil). It has power, wealth,[1] security, and offers every person who steps foot on its soil the opportunity to pursue, and achieve, the American Dream.[2] But it is not without flaws. With such greatness comes sacrifice; sacrifice by each and every American, or at least that portion of America which helps contribute to its greatness. For most Americans, ignorance is bliss in this respect. That is, they blindly accept their role in America because they are not aware of any other possible life. For the minority of Americans who are unfortunate to find

---

[1] Wealth is a subjective term which will be used interchangeably herein. In this instance, it means the accumulation of monetary assets.

[2] A strong argument can be made that the "American Dream" was created by the government, corporations and banks as a means to keep the average American shackled to a job and city that they could never escape as a result of buying a home that would financially handicap them for the rest of their lives. The same goes for going to college (literally incurring a lifetime of debt) and also the American school system in general. For example, ever wonder why American schools rarely, if ever, teach financial literacy, how to do your taxes, how to prepare a healthy (or any) meal, and instead force children to learn useless skills such as algebra and ancient Greek mythology (hello Icarus!).

themselves at or below the poverty line (approximately ten percent),[3] their destiny is largely chosen for them, for their constant struggle to stay afloat prevents them from seeking or knowing any other way of life. On the other end of spectrum, for the minority of Americans who are fortunate enough to classify themselves as being in the upper class (approximately 1-2%),[4] they are free to choose their own path, though sadly, many continue with their same benign existence, the value and quality of which is largely debated in this book.

For the vast majority of Americans, however, who fall into the ever-growing middle class, however you choose to define it, they are the ones to whom this book is directed. For they, unlike the lower class who are shackled by poverty, are more like the upper class in that they too are free to choose their own destiny. Yet, whereas the upper class has the luxury of being frivolous without real financial consequences, the middle class, like those in poverty, often find themselves in a constant struggle for survival.

But the middle class are in a far better position than those in poverty because they have alternative solutions for finding happiness. Yet, for reasons explained further in this book, their destiny, like those in poverty, is also largely chosen for them simply because they are unaware of those other alternatives. This, my friends, is solely an American paradox. For only Americans remain naive to the endless opportunities which abound. Opportunities which other developed countries have embraced for years, enriching the lives of their citizens in the process.

---

[3] http://en.wikipedia.org/wiki/Poverty_in_the_United_States (according to the U.S. Census Bureau from 2020 based on a U.S. population of 331 million people at the time). The poverty level for 2021 was set at $27,700 (total yearly income) for a family of four. *Id.*

[4] http://en.wikipedia.org/wiki/American_upper_class.

As Americans, we are taught from very early on to work hard so that we can provide for our family and live a life of financial comfort. And while hard work is certainly the backbone of any successful entity, be it a country, a company, or even an individual, America is the only successful country in the world that doesn't properly reward its citizens for their hard-working efforts. For most middle to upper class Americans, their typical path is as follows: graduate from college and move to a big city for a few years, get married, have a baby, move to the suburbs (likely within a few miles of where they were born and where most of their friends and family still live and have similarly never left for an extended period of time), have another baby or two, and all the while, at least for the primary breadwinner if not both parents, work 50 hours/week, 50 weeks/year for the rest of their lives until retirement, all so that you can afford the aforementioned lifestyle. And while that may be a perfectly fulfilling life for many Americans, for most, it's the only life they know exists. This book, however, is meant to apprise you of the countless other possible ways to live your life.

Although, as you will see in this book, the alternative path I have chosen in life revolves around world travel, that's not necessarily to say that travel has to be the alternative path for everyone. Rather, it can be anything that brings you more joy than spending the vast majority of your life at a job that most Americans simply don't enjoy. For me, after practicing law at two of the largest law firms in the world for eight years, I quit my job in 2013 to travel the world with my then wife. We lived and worked in Bangkok, Thailand as English teachers (and I also taught at their law school) at an international university, but had summers off so we traveled every summer for three consecutive months for four consecutive summers. But that was my story. There are countless ways to spend your life and money other than the aforementioned typical American way. My way is just one story. I invite and encourage you to find yours.

At a relatively young age (now forty-four, but thirty-three when I set off on my world traveling adventures and began writing this book), I have been fortunate to travel extensively throughout the world. I've been to approximately seventy countries on six different continents (all but Antarctica which I expect to visit before I die, along with the Moon/space if/when that becomes more economically feasible, as it's already become a tourism industry so now it's just a matter of price). Among the many common themes I've noticed throughout my travels, the one that stands out the most is that Americans are the only successful,[5] first-world citizens that don't travel extensively outside of their home country. Time after time, I meet Australians, Canadians and citizens of every first-world European country (e.g., Germans, British, French, Austrians, Dutch, Swedish, Spanish, Italians, Scandinavians, etc.) that travel for weeks, months, and even years at a time. Americans, on the other hand, the few times you do see them abroad, rarely ever travel for more than a week or two at a time.

Part of this is due to the fact that America in and of itself is a huge country, approximately 2.5 times the size of Europe,[6] and so traveling from state to state is, at least geographically, the equivalent of traveling from one country to another in Europe. Another reason why Americans travel outside their home country less than any other first-world nation is

---

[5] Like "wealth," success is also a subjective term which is used interchangeably herein. This particular use is meant to imply monetary wealth. But my personal favorite definition of it is how Tony Robbins defines it: success is being able to do whatever you want, whenever you want, within reason at least. In fact, whereas the old status symbols of success were a fancy car, big house and nice watch, the new "flex" is freedom—time freedom, financial freedom and location freedom, all of which I've been able to achieve in the last several years.
[6] www.ielanguages.com/esl/usvseurope.doc ("The area of the United States (including Alaska and Hawaii) is 9,161,923 km2, while the area of Europe is 3,788,027 km2").

because of their ignorance and ego (i.e., they think that America is the greatest country on Earth and every other country pales in comparison).

The main reason, however, why Americans travel outside of their home country less than any other first-world nation is simple: whereas almost every other successful, first-world country rewards its citizens with four, six, or sometimes even eight to twelve weeks of holiday per year, Americans typically only receive one to two weeks of vacation per year. In fact, according to a recent study by the U.S. Bureau of Labor Statistics, the average full-time American employee only received 8.1 days of vacation after one year on the job.[7] After an astounding twenty-five years on the job, that figure increases to 15.7.[8] In fact, of the twenty richest nations that were the subject of the aforementioned study, only Japan fared worse in terms of the average number of paid vacation and holidays its workers receive per year.[9] Of course, Japan literally has a word ("karoshi") for working yourself to death, so query whether that's the country we should aspire to be.

One of the reasons for this is because in most first-world countries, there is a law that states its workers are legally required to take a minimum number of vacation days per year.[10] In France, for example, the global vacation leader, its workers are required to take at least thirty days of vacation per year.[11] In Austria and Portugal, when including holidays, its citizens are *required* to take thirty-five days off a year.[12] In the United States, however, no such law exists. In fact, out

---

[7] http://theweek.com/article/index/244771/americas-war-on-vacation-by-the-numbers.

[8] *Id.*

[9] *Id.*

[10] http://www.thrillist.com/travel/nation/paid-time-off-which-countries-get-the-most-vacation-time.

[11] http://theweek.com/article/index/244771/americas-war-on-vacation-by-the-numbers.

[12] *Id.*

of the twenty-one developed nations which were the subject of the aforementioned study, the United States was the *only* one where its workers were not guaranteed paid vacation.[13] Rather, vacation time is left solely to the discretion of the employer. What's even more shocking, however, is that even when Americans are permitted by their employers to take vacation, they often don't. For example, according to the aforementioned study, 57% of American workers had unused vacation time, totaling approximately 175 million unused vacation days.[14] This is likely due to the fact that even when Americans are afforded vacation, they're often too scared to take it for fear of being looked down upon by their peers or even demoted or fired by their supervisor.

By way of example, Richard Branson, founder and CEO of Virgin Group, recently announced a new policy for all of his United States and United Kingdom employees whereby they're permitted to take an unlimited number of vacation days, provided they get their work done.[15] However, while this may sound great in theory for Virgin Group employees, many people are speculating that the end result will be that employees actually end up taking less vacation than they otherwise would have under an ordinary vacation policy, for fear of not knowing how the policy works or if and when it's appropriate to take a vacation. Branson's description of the policy in his new book certainly doesn't help quench any of those fears: "It is left to the employee to decide if and when he or she feels like taking a few hours, a day, a week or a month off, the assumption being that they are only going to do it when they feel a hundred percent comfortable ... that their absence will not in any way damage the business -- or,

---

[13] *Id.*

[14] *Id.*

[15] http://www.entrepreneur.com/article/237783.

for that matter, their careers."[16] 100% comfortable? When has anyone ever felt 100% comfortable about anything, ever?

Another classic illustration of how Americans rarely take advantage of vacation time, even when it's available, is when Americans change jobs in corporate America. Typically, they only take one to two weeks off work before beginning their next employment, and sometimes they take as little as a few days (or just the weekend). Often times, these people have been at their jobs for several or more years, and will likely remain at their next job for the same amount of time, or more. Yet, they only allow themselves a couple of weeks (or less) before jumping right back into the saddle. I was always amazed when, as a corporate lawyer at two of the largest law firms in the world, I would often see departure emails from my colleagues (typically sent out on a Friday afternoon), and they would generally go something like this: "Thanks to everyone I've worked with for helping me become a better lawyer over these past [x] years…Starting on Monday, my new contact information is as follows…"

As described further below, as a lawyer at some of the largest/most prestigious law firms in the world, associates typically make anywhere from $200,000-250,000/year, before bonus. For the life of me, I must have seen hundreds of emails like the above sent out by my colleagues during the approximately eight years I worked in big firm law (prior to moving to Asia). Every time, it amazed me when I saw people leaving the job that they had worked at for the past few or more years, presumably saving tens if not hundreds of thousands of dollars in the process, and before doing it all over again, they were only taking a few days or at most a couple of weeks off to enjoy the fruits of their labor. In fact, I recently recall a friend from college posting something on

---

[16] http://www.huffingtonpost.com/2014/09/23/virgin-unlimited-vacation_n_5869708.html.

Facebook to the effect of: "Officially unemployed for the next 70 hours! Thanks for the last 11 years, X! [X being one of the largest financial consulting firms in the world]. It's been quite the ride, but looking forward to the next chapter:)."

This woman had been working probably 50-60 hours/week, 50 weeks/year for the last eleven years, undoubtedly making hundreds of thousands of dollars, and her reward for her efforts was a mere 70 hours of vacation time, before presumably starting another eleven-year stretch. Needless to say, as explained further below, when I finally decided to call it quits from big firm law, my departure email was a little different. And surprisingly, the reaction I was received was almost universally positive (and of course envious).

The result of all of the above is the ultimate paradox: Americans, perhaps the most successful citizens in the world, also remain some of the most deprived. For vacation allows you to spend your time doing things you are passionate about. It also allows you to educate yourself about things that you may not know or have the time to learn about. Or for some, it's simply a time to recharge your batteries to prepare yourself for the rigors of work that lie ahead, often making you more productive when you return to work. As for the woman who was the subject of my above story, she had two small children. At a minimum, you would think she would have wanted to spend a couple of weeks with her kids before jumping back into the rat race. Apparently not.

Of course, I realize that were it not for the fact that Americans take far fewer vacation days and holidays per year than any almost any other successful, first-world country in the world, we would not be where we are today: that is, the most powerful and "successful" country in the world. But as alluded to above, that success and power comes at a great price. A price paid by each and every working-class citizen. And contrary to what you may think, the purpose of this book is not to dissuade you from continuing down this road of hard work and little play, but rather, to educate you as to the endless world of opportunity which exists outside of the corporate rat race that most Americans find themselves in. A rat race which, for most Americans, is the only race they know exists.

Part One
The Conceptual Recognition Stage

Approximately 10% of Americans despise their jobs while another 42% merely tolerate them. This means that during a typical work week, approximately 52% of Americans spend 75% of their time awake doing something they despise or merely tolerate, all so they can spend the remaining 25% doing something they actually enjoy.

Recognizing, at least conceptually, the rat race that the typical American lives in, often requires two steps. The first is the recognition that time is money. As the expression goes, life is short. Therefore, as Marc Cuban, owner of the Dallas Mavericks and one of the most successful businessmen in the United States likes to say, time is the most valuable asset you possess. After you've come to grips with that reality, consider the following:

Time is Money

America is a peculiar place. When it comes to people's job satisfaction, I like to categorize people into three different groups. First, are the hundred million or more Americans (approximately 42%) [11] who do not enjoy their jobs, but merely tolerate them. By "enjoy," I mean getting satisfaction the majority of your work days, and not despising the thought

---

[11] http://www.marketplace.org/topics/economy/attitude-check/most-americans-feel-satisfied-their-jobs.

of going into work almost every day, particularly on Mondays for those majority of Americans who work Monday through Friday and play hard enough on the weekends so as to give them enough inertia to make it through the following week (aka weekend warriors).

The second category of American workers are the small minority (approximately 10%)[2] that truly despise their job, but for various reasons (e.g., financial hardship, family commitments, etc.) have no other choice (or so they think) but to suffer through it each and every day. This group varies slightly from the aforementioned group in that they don't tolerate their jobs (typically 40-50 hours per week, 5 days a week, if not more) for the sake of being able to enjoy their two days of freedom a week, a conscious choice albeit one which I would argue is made without being fully cognizant of all available options. Rather, this second group of American workers suffers through their jobs simply because they have no other viable options, a predicament often brought upon themselves through, often unnecessary, over commitment, as discussed further below.

The third group of American workers (approximately 48%)[3] actually enjoy their jobs and don't dread the thought of going into work each and every day, particularly on Mondays for the typical American worker.

For those Americans that find themselves in the unfortunate second group that truly despise their jobs but are unable to change their fate due to various, often self-imposed conditions, this book will likely offer little guidance. For the 48% of Americans who *purportedly*[4] claim to like their jobs, this book may still enlighten you to other possible ways to live your life. For even if you enjoy your job, you likely

---

[2] *Id.*

[3] *Id.*

[4] In all likelihood, many of the job satisfaction surveys are conducted by employers and so the veracity of their results is questionable at best.

enjoy your free time far more. And as explained further below, your free time is the most valuable asset you possess. For the last group of American workers, however (the 42% who don't enjoy their jobs but tolerate them simply because they're unaware of the multitude of alternative options available at their disposal), you are the target audience for this book. At best, I hope this book provides you with the impetus and tools necessary to change your life for the better. At worst, I hope this book enlightens you as to those alternative options for finding happiness in this world, so that even if you continue to live your life like the millions of Americans who merely tolerate, but don't actually enjoy their daily existence, at least you're doing so fully cognizant of all of the other options available to you. For as a wise saying goes, "happiness should not be a destination. It should be a way of life."

Before delving into what I like to call the "Conceptual Recognition Stage" of this life-changing process, we need to step back and examine what it is that this book is attempting to change for the better: the average American's daily existence. For the approximate 42% of Americans who do not like what they do for a living but tolerate it for a mere two days of freedom and also because they are unaware of other possible ways to live their life (and even for the 48% that enjoy their jobs but could be doing something they enjoy far more), we need to examine how it is that the average American spends their day in the ordinary working world.

Assuming the typical 40-50 hour work week, 5 days a week,[5] the average American worker wakes up between 6

---

[5] This of course does not account for those Americans who are "fortunate" (or unfortunate depending on how you view it) enough to land jobs with large law firms and/or financial institutions, which typically require their employees to work 60-70 (and often more) hours per week. And while they are often handsomely compensated (at least monetarily) for their efforts, as this book explains, those efforts are often at the

and 7 am every workday, spends the first hour or so of their day getting ready for work, the next hour or two of their day getting to work and settled in at work (e.g., getting their morning coffee, checking email and their favorite daily websites, etc.), and the next eight or nine hours at work.[6] If lucky, the average American worker gets 30-60 minutes of free time during the day for lunch, which is typically spent at their desk attending to personal matters, running errands close by their office/home, or in rare instances, working out. After finishing their workday, the typical American worker spends the next hour or two coming home from and decompressing from work (e.g., checking the daily mail, changing from work clothes to comfy clothes, having an alcoholic beverage or working out, etc.). All told, this leaves the average American worker with approximately two to three hours of free time per day (from approximately 7 to 10 pm), during which they also need to eat dinner.

For the single worker, this "free" time is typically spent working out or watching their favorite television shows. Or perhaps going on a date in an effort to achieve greater personal happiness. For those with families, this time is undoubtedly spent attending to family matters, such as making dinner and/or lunch for their kids, helping kids with their homework, or just generally enjoying family time.

On the weekends, the average American worker spends at least one of their two weekend days running errands and catching up on all of the personal things they were unable to

---

expense of great personal satisfaction, often times resulting in catastrophic life-changing events, such as divorce, child estrangement, alcoholism or other substance abuses, obesity etc.

[6] This book was originally written during my world travels between 2013 and 2016, prior to Covid-19. While Covid-19 has obviously changed the work landscape, particularly with respect to remote work and potentially forever, the general principles in this book remain the same and to the extent they've changed, this book has been updated to reflect such changes.

attend to during the week (e.g., doing laundry, cleaning dishes, grocery shopping, attending to household matters, etc.). This leaves the average American worker with approximately one day per week to spend however they choose. For many Americans, this time is often spent simply lounging around the house because they are too exhausted from the rest of the week to do anything that requires the exertion of extra energy.

In a typical week, if an average American sleeps eight hours per night (likely a very conservative figure), they are awake 112 hours per week. Combining all of the above (i.e., 2-3 hours of free time per weekday and one weekend day/night free), the average American worker is left with approximately 26 to 31 hours of free time per week, which equates to approximately 23 to 28% of their time being awake. The rest of their time (approximately 72-77%) is spent either at work or getting ready for/decompressing from work and getting to/from work.

Combining these stats with the earlier quality of life/job satisfaction statistics we looked at earlier in this book, this means that 42% of Americans spend approximately 75% of their waking life doing something they do not enjoy but merely tolerate, all so they can spend the remaining 25% doing something they actually enjoy (and for the 48% of Americans that claim to like their job, query whether they like it enough to spend 75% of their waking life doing it). To me, these figures are staggering. As one CEO of a progressive company recently put it when describing why so many companies were having difficulty getting employees to come back to work following 1.5 years of Covid-19 lockdowns: "I don't think we've fully reckoned with how the pandemic crystallized for people how much they hate their job. It's not just that people are lazy or don't want to get

Covid at work. They don't want to slowly kill themselves by wasting their life at a soul-sucking job."[7]

Even more, assuming the typical American worker receives two weeks of paid vacation per year (a big assumption, for as explained earlier, the U.S. is the only developed country in the world that doesn't legally guarantee its workers paid vacation, meaning it's often left to the employer's discretion), in a 52-week year, this equates to 4% of the year. In other words, the typical American worker spends 96% of the year engaged in the typical work week (during which they have 25% of their waking time to spend doing the things they enjoy doing), all so that they can spend 4% of the year completely enjoying the things they like to do, without any of the concerns/hassles of their daily working life.[8]

And the greatest irony of all, is that for those Americans who are "fortunate" enough to procure jobs with some of America's highest paying companies, those numbers are even more skewed. In other words, in America, the more money you make typically means the less time you have to enjoy spending that money doing the things you actually enjoying doing. This particularly holds true for those jobs where your salary is directly tied to the number of hours you're required to work. For lawyers, this is often referred to as "billable hours," though a more appropriate term would be "sweat equity," because your ability to earn equity is directly tied to the amount of sweat you're required to expend ("sweat" being a relative term, of course, because in reality these high earners often have little, if any, time to engage in physical

---

[7] Dan Price, CEO of Gravity Payments.

[8] In reality, even during those two weeks of vacation, the average American, or at least office worker, at a minimum, is still checking their work email/voicemail and often times still doing work so as not to be too overwhelmed when they return to their daily working life and also for fear of being viewed poorly by their superiors and/or peers.

6

exercise resulting in sweat, but rather are sitting at a desk the majority of their workdays). As someone once put it to me, "making partner at a law firm is like winning a pie eating contest...and the prize is more pie."

Compared to other successful, first-world countries, their employees typically receive up to four weeks of paid vacation and rarely work more than forty hours per week.[9] In fact, in Europe, many countries have adopted a thirty-five hour standard work week.[10] Moreover, in my experience working with lawyers (arguably some of the hardest workers) from Europe, during the months of July and August, very little business gets done as most employees take a month or even two off to spend time with their families before their kids return to school. An analogy I like to draw, though a vast topic in its own right and thus likely the subject of another, separate book, occurs when I often find myself confounded by listening to single people describe the attributes they're looking for in a spouse.

For me, once I came to the recognition that time is the most valuable asset I own, finding the attributes I was looking for in someone was simple, though finding someone who possessed them was anything but. But the attributes themselves were simple to identify: find the person who enjoys doing the same things you enjoy doing during the 25% of our waking lives which we're able to spend doing whatever it is that we like to do.[11] If you don't, then you're forced to break down that percentage even further because you're spending part of that time doing the things that your spouse enjoys, even if you do not.

---

[9]

https://en.wikipedia.org/wiki/List_of_minimum_annual_leave_by_country.

[10] *Id.*

[11] This was of course before I was able to reach the Pulling the Trigger Stage which is the subject of the next chapter discussed below.

The analogy I often see which confounds me occurs when people try to find their spouse, and it goes as follows: religion versus eating habits. Being Jewish (though not a practicing Jew and frankly I'm Atheist), I have many Jewish friends. Of those friends, the large majority insist on marrying someone who is Jewish. Yet, like me, they are not religious and religion is not a part of their daily lives. Yet, many of these people who are carnivorous and are willing to eat almost anything, would have no problem marrying a vegetarian.

Using my mantra that time is the most valuable attribute you possess, I often ask them how often in a 365-day year religion comes up in their daily routine. The answer, almost universally, is 3-4 days per year (typically the High Holidays, Rosh Hashanah and Yom Kippur, and Passover; maybe a few days of Chanukah if you're really religious or have kids). Conversely, if you're a carnivore or even an omnivore, how often would your partner being a vegetarian (let alone a vegan or someone who keeps kosher) become an issue in your daily life?

The answer, again almost universally, is always the same: every single day, and often several times in a day if you eat multiple meals together in a typical day (e.g., at dinner when you want chicken parmesan and your spouse wants eggplant parmesan, or even at breakfast when you want a sausage or bacon omelet and your spouse wants a spinach omelet, or no omelet at all if he/she is vegan). The point is, once you come to the recognition that time is the most valuable asset you own, why would you ever purposely limit yourself to someone who possesses an attribute which you don't share which you know will be a recurring, daily issue for you for the rest of your life (e.g., one of you being a carnivore or omnivore and the other being a vegetarian, vegan or keeping kosher)? Equally surprising, why would you ever limit yourself to approximately 3% of the population (the Jewish population in the U.S., which would have been 10% were it not for the Holocaust) for an attribute which will only be an issue 3-4 days per year? Yet time and time again, I'm confronted with people who consciously engage in such behavior, and not surprisingly, either continue to remain single, or worse, end up marrying the wrong person.

Having now hopefully recognized the concept of time being the most valuable asset you possess (the first part in the process of what I like to call the "Conceptual Recognition Stage"), it's time to move onto the second part of the Conceptual Recognition process.

How Much You Make is Simply a Function of How Much You Spend

Even after one comes to grips with the conceptual reality that time is money, it still may take weeks, months, or even years, if ever, for a person to get comfortable with the idea of escaping the rat race that consumes most Americans. Typically, it takes a catastrophic event in a person's life (e.g., death of a parent, spouse or child, or more recently, the Covid-19 pandemic) for that person to reevaluate what is most important. Short of such an event, it is extremely difficult, if not impossible, for the typical American to come to terms with the idea of leaving a relatively comfortable lifestyle for the unknown, even when that unknown presents opportunities for happiness leaps and bounds beyond what the average American ever experiences.

For me, that catastrophic event took place when my father died in November 2007. He was 63 at the time, the same age as his father (my paternal grandfather) when he died. By the time my father died, he had been divorced twice and had four children (myself included), two with each of his two wives. He had several careers over the course of his life, most notably as a lawyer and a commercial real estate broker. As a

9

lawyer, he began his career as a criminal defense attorney. After receiving one too many death threats from clients whom he was unable to keep out of jail, he moved over to divorce law. After two divorces, presumably he decided that maybe divorce law was not for him either.

Up until he was almost 50, my father had spent his entire life in Illinois, in particular the Chicagoland area. He went to grade school, high school, college and law school in Illinois, and spent the first twenty or so years of his career practicing law in Chicago. Shortly before he turned 50, however, his brother, also an attorney in Chicago (a federal prosecutor) moved to Los Angeles to start a pizza restaurant with a fellow attorney from Los Angeles. Years later, that pizza restaurant would become one of the most successful casual-dining restaurant chains in America. Knowing my father was not enamored with his legal career in Chicago, his brother offered him the opportunity to take charge of all the commercial real estate development for his new pizza venture. At the time, his enterprise had probably less than ten restaurants across the country. Their goal, however, was to reach over fifty restaurants (and eventually hundreds) in the next five to ten years, and my father was asked to take charge of that endeavor.

One of the few reasons my father liked being a lawyer was that he could be his own boss (he always worked as a solo practitioner or with a few other partners with whom he was close friends). Thus, although he would now be working for a small company, he figured since his brother was one of the two founders, he would enjoy the same autonomy he enjoyed during his legal career.[12]

---

[12] This may have held true were it not for the fact that my uncle and his partner sold their enterprise to a Fortune 500 company shortly after my father moved to LA. And while my father was able to maintain his position with his brother's pizza venture notwithstanding its subsequent acquisition, suddenly he found himself working for a Fortune 500

My father was always someone who enjoyed the finer things in life. From luxury automobiles to state-of-the-art electronics to nice houses to the newest gadgets money could buy, my father certainly lived life to the fullest. His fatal flaw, however (besides cancer which ultimately took his life), was that he often lived beyond his means. By way of example, at the time my father died, he made more money than he ever made in his career, legal or otherwise.[13] The year he died, he made approximately $500,000 per year. Unfortunately, he was spending more. With four kids, two ex-wives, and a panache for the finest things in life, no matter how much money he made, he simply couldn't keep up with his financial commitments, obligatory or otherwise.

Three of the most vivid memories I have about my father and his financial struggles are as follows. The first took place when I was about ten years old. Like most children of divorce, I saw my father every Wednesday night and every other weekend (until he moved to LA). One Wednesday night, when I was about to head out for dinner with my father, my mother, so often (and rightfully so) frustrated by his lack of financial responsibility, both generally and specifically for me, nonchalantly asked me to remind him he was several or more months behind in his child support payments. I imagine she did this because we were likely headed out for a nice dinner, an activity for which my father typically spared little expense.

In retort, I explained to my mother that although I was terribly sorry for my father's financial shortcomings, if I had to choose between a father who was financially derelict but

company, rather than for his brother.

[13] After doing commercial real estate exclusively for his brother's venture for the first ten or so years after he moved to LA, he eventually joined a small commercial real estate practice before venturing out on his own, though he continued to focus on large chain restaurants, with his brother's chain remaining one of his most steadfast clients.

emotionally wanted to be a part of my life, versus a fiscally responsible father who didn't want to be a part of my life, I would choose the former every time. I think I even said something to the effect of I want him to be able to see me walk down the aisle on my wedding day and also to see his grandchildren, the irony being that he died before either of those events could take place. Notwithstanding the foregoing, my relationship with my father drastically changed later in life once I became financially independent and no longer needed his monetary support. After that time, I began to view my father more like a friend than a father figure, as we enjoyed many of the finer things in life which he always enjoyed, together (e.g., golf trips, ski trips, trips to Vegas, steak dinners, fine wine, cigars, etc.).

The second story I recall which evidences my father's financial shortcomings took place on one of our several ski trips, this one to Aspen, Colorado. I recall we went to a fancy sushi restaurant (is there any other kind in Aspen?) and my little half-sister, probably around 7 at the time, wanted to order a single piece of sashimi for around $30. This caused quite the little stir amongst my father and my stepmom at the time, but ultimately, as was so often the case, my father gave in and my sister received her $30 piece of sashimi, which clearly didn't suffice as her meal. Needless to say, no seven-year old child (or anyone for that matter) needs a single piece of sashimi for $30.

The third and final story which evidences my father's cavalier attitude towards money took place immediately upon moving to LA. Rather than taking a prudent approach with a new career and purchasing a modest home in a modest neighborhood, my father immediately purchased a $1.2 million home in Tarzana, one of the five boroughs of the bourgeoisie San Fernando Valley. Even worse, however, he neglected to purchase earthquake insurance, a mistake which financially crippled him when an earthquake struck within a year of purchasing the home.[14]

At this point in the book you're probably wondering what is the purpose of my sharing intimate details about my relationship with my father. The answer is twofold. First, as described above, even after coming to terms with the concept that time is money, I firmly believe that it takes a personal, catastrophic event in a person's life before they are able to internalize this universal truth. For me, that event was my father's death at the age of 63. I was twenty-seven at the time. Even more shocking, however, was recognizing for the first time that my father's father also died at the age of 63, literally within three weeks of the same age as my father when he passed. Second, and more generally applicable for purposes of educating the readers of this book, my father's financial shortcomings taught me a valuable life lesson which goes to the very heart of the message of this book, one that is equally as important as the "time is money" mantra. That message is simple: how much money you make is simply a function of how much you spend.

As suggested above, at the time my father died, he was making approximately $500,000 a year, a salary that likely put him in the top 1% of all wage earners in America. Yet, despite this, he continued to live beyond his means, and died with virtually nothing in his savings. No human being, no matter how many kids you have and no matter how grand your lifestyle, should need more than $500,000 a year. Yet,

---

[14] As a comic aside, the home he purchased was the childhood home of a then famous child TV star. Even more amazing, on my first trip to LA to visit my father and to see his new home, I sat directly next to that child star (a few years older than me at the time) on my flight out there. Even more surprising, the child star was flying in coach with me while his father flew first class. When I asked what his father did, he replied, "he's my manager." Though I didn't say it, all I could think was maybe it's time for a new manager.

for my father, that figure was not enough. And the reason is simply because he lived beyond his means. As a small example, every single morning he would buy a Venti Starbucks coffee, without fail. In contrast, I make coffee every morning, as well as breakfast, lunch and most often dinner too, whenever I'm not traveling that is 😊.

By way of comparison, and as explained further in the section below, before I left my big law firm lifestyle, I was making approximately $250,000 per year. However, I was also living in New York City and consequently paying close to $3,000 a month in rent. With a monthly income of approximately $10,000 (after taxes), I was spending approximately 30% of my income on rent, a figure which generally put me in good shape as compared to the rest of the American working population. Thus, even while living in NYC, I was still able to save approximately $5,000 per month, due in part to my hefty salary but also in part because of my saving nature, which I likely would not have had were it not for seeing my father's financial struggles.

On the other end of the spectrum but also by way of comparison, when I took a job as a teacher at an international university in Thailand from 2013-2016, I was making approximately $1,200 a month (with no taxes, a significant factor as discussed further below). Prior to being told I would be receiving free housing, I looked up the average cost of living in Bangkok, Thailand, where I knew I'd be teaching, and the average monthly rent was approximately $300-500, which meant I'd continue to spend approximately one-third of my income on rent. The point is that although my monthly salary as a teacher in Thailand was approximately 10% of what I made as a lawyer in NYC, due to the cost of living adjustment, my cost of housing (compared to my salary), was more or less the same. Similarly, whereas the average meal in NYC costs anywhere from $10-25, the average cost of a meal in Thailand, at the time at least, was $1-3, again the same proportion to my salary adjustment, approximately 10%.

14

Thus, while nominally speaking I was making significantly less in Thailand than what I was making in NYC, due to the cost of living adjustment, my lifestyle remained the same (i.e., still in the top 10% of all wage earners).

The point of all of this is that, how much money you make is simply a function of how much you spend. For my father, no matter how much he made, he always found a way to spend more. For me, I have never been able to live that way, but rather, have always been a saver (and more recently investor). Thus, for some of you who are reading this book and are like my father, the lessons described herein will likely be of little use to you. But for those of you who have been able to live within your means, if you so choose, know that there's another way to find happiness out there for you that doesn't involve working 50 hours/week, 50 weeks/year at a job you don't like or merely tolerate (as an aside, my father actually enjoyed his last career as a commercial real estate broker, but nevertheless continued to live beyond his means). Before achieving that happiness, however you first must recognize the two aforementioned altruisms: time is money and how much you make is simply a function of how much you spend.

Part Two
The Personal Recognition Stage

I have several regrets in my life but only when it comes to my career, which was deciding to begin it at a prestigious, international law firm in Chicago, rather than a boutique entertainment law firm in Los Angeles, the latter of which potentially could have provided me with a path to becoming an entertainment lawyer, something I always aspired to be. After regretting that decision for years, I promised myself that if I was ever presented with another life-changing opportunity, this time I would take the riskier choice with the higher upside.

My entire life, all I ever thought about was making money. Likely in large part a result of seeing my father struggle financially his entire life (again, only in terms of his ability, or inability, to live within his means, not in terms of his annual income). But regardless of the reasons, my goal in life, ever since I can remember, was never to have to worry about money. And by never worrying about money, I merely mean being able to buy anything within reason without worrying about the financial consequences. I don't need a jet, a yacht, or even a 2nd home (though the latter I've since come to learn is actually a liability, rather than an asset, unless you make money on it by renting it out when you're not using it which is my new plan in life; more on that below). But by never having to worry about money, I simply mean the simple luxuries in life (a roof over my head, a mode of transportation, going out for a decent meal once or twice a week, etc.). I never wanted to have to look at a menu and wonder whether I should get a certain dish or not (single pieces of $30 sashimi aside).

As a result of this way of thinking, I have always been financially risk averse. The irony, of course, is that socially, I'm a huge risk taker. Be it eating exotic things (e.g., dog in Vietnam, live octopus in Korea, killing a chicken for dinner in a village in the Philippines), engaging in "extra-curricular" activities, climbing mountains/volcanoes, trekking through jungles, partaking in extreme adventure sports (e.g., skydiving, bungee jumping, hang gliding, scuba diving, downhill mountain biking, extreme skiing, etc.), I like to joke that if there's not a small chance of death involved in the activity, I'll likely be bored by it.

But in terms of my financial aversion to risk, it has dictated almost every path I've taken in life, up until my recent life-changing decisions, of course. Starting with elementary school, though that choice was made for me, my parents[1] sent me to a Chicago Public School for kindergarten through 8th grade. After that, although I was admitted to one of the most prestigious high school programs in the country (the international baccalaureate, or IB, program), I decided to attend a private kindergarten through 12th grade school in Lincoln Park, Chicago (the affluent neighborhood where I was fortunate to grow up, though I also grew up just a couple of blocks away from one of the most dangerous neighborhoods in the country at the time, Cabrini Green), in large part because my sister also went to that school and was a senior by the time I arrived.[2]

---

[1] Parents hereinafter refers to my mom and stepdad, for despite having a biological father, my stepfather essentially raised (and supported) me from five years old, a fact for which I am forever indebted to him for the rest of my life and his, beyond any measure.

[2] In my juvenile view, if my parents were going to pay approximately $10,000 per year (now an astonishing $30,000 per year) to send my sister to private high school, I wanted to be afforded that same opportunity.

I have very mixed feelings about my high school. On the one hand, I received an excellent high school education which helped me get admitted to the University of Illinois ("U of I") and also helped prepare me for the rigorous academic challenges that lay ahead. On the other hand, my high school cost more than my college (including room and board at college which is crazy) and consequently I had to take out student loans (more on that discussed below) to help pay for college and then law school. But in hindsight, financially, going to my high school may have been a blessing in disguise. For had I gone to the IB Program at a Chicago Public School like most of my intelligent/hard-working peers from my grade school, I likely would have been admitted to Ivy League (or Ivy League caliber) schools like Harvard, Yale, or Stanford, and thus would have incurred even more student loan debt than I incurred by going to the U of I, a public state school.[3]

But putting aside the financial ramifications of going to my high school, the biggest negative takeaway was the social aspect of it. Simply put, it was an elitist school where the majority of students have a false sense of reality. The two biggest anecdotal stories I recall from my high school days which epitomize the school environment are as follows, both of which took place during my senior year in high school.

The first involves the college application process. For its own self-serving reasons, my high school likes to send its students to two types of schools: the first are Ivy League and Ivy League caliber schools, which if you have the ability to get in and, more importantly, the means to afford it *without*

Little did I know that that decision would result in my paying for half of my college education, and enduring a less than socially desirable high school experience.

[3] Also discussed further below is the merit of going to prestigious Ivy League (or Ivy League caliber) schools as opposed to public institutions, particularly when the result is more accumulated tuition debt.

jeopardizing your financial future, is hard to argue against. The second type of school my high school likes to send its students to, however, are tiny liberal arts schools, not on par with their larger Ivy League counterparts, except with respect to tuition costs. Schools like Middlebury, Haverford, Vassar, Swarthmore, Oberlin, Tufts, Miami of Ohio, Washington University in St. Louis, etc. My personal theory as to why students from my high school tend to flock to these schools is because, ultimately, they're an extension of my high school: tiny schools where students can remain a big fish in a small pond and remain oblivious to the reality that exists outside of that pond/bubble.

My high school had approximately 65 students per class year, a shockingly low number for a school that resides in the heart of Chicago. As a result, students who attend my high school tend to prefer the big fish, small pond environment for college as well, and thus flock to schools with relatively low enrollment sizes, typically 5,000 students or less.

On rare occasion, a student from my high school will attend a major university (e.g., 30,000+ students), but significantly, that university will almost never be the U of I, the flagship public state school for the State of Illinois and a fraction of the cost compared with private institutions or even other state schools.[4] Even more shocking, in the rare instance where a student from my high school attended a major university, it was often inferior academically to (or at least on par with) the much more affordable U of I. For example, students from my high school have been known to go to the University of Colorado, Vermont, University of Santa Barbara, Emory, the aforementioned Washington University in St. Louis, or even Indiana University or the University of Wisconsin. And while some of those schools have enrollment

---

[4] I should state that this was all true at the time I went there from 1994-1998 and while it's possible things have changed since, I suspect for the most part they have not.

sizes similar to that of the U of I, none are superior academically, at least not superior like an Ivy League school where, if accepted, you can at least make an argument for spending four or more times as much money on an education than by going to the state public school.

As an example of the above, the year I graduated high school in 1998, not only was I the only student to attend the U of I, a statistic shocking in its own right, but I was also the only male student to even submit an application. And rest assured, with its prestigious pedigree and lack of student interest, the majority of my peers would have surely been admitted to U of I had they submitted an application, but as discussed above, either for fear of being a small fish in a big pond or fear of being looked down upon by their peers, my classmates fled to collegiate extensions of our high school, or alternatively other large universities, inferior or on par academically to the U of I, but significantly costlier.

The second anecdotal story I recall about my high school which is indicative of its elitist nature also has to do with my senior year of high school, this time involving my graduation ceremony. Whereas most high schools announce their graduating class either alphabetically, randomly, or in some other egalitarian form, my high school, at least at the time, chose to announce its graduating class in ascending order, based on the number of years you attended the school.

Now recall that my high school is also a kindergarten through 12th grade school. Thus, many of the students, approximately a third or even half, have attended the same school since kindergarten (known as the "12 Year Gang"). Consequently, these students are announced separately after all other students have been announced. What makes this process even more unfathomable, however, is the level of enthusiasm which rises with each new class year announced, both by the MC and by the audience. I often akin it to the announcement of the starting lineup for the Chicago Bulls, with the last group of students being the equivalent of

Michael Jordan or Derrick Rose (when Derrick Rose was a healthy superstar, that is). In reality, as I'm sure you've surmised, what the MC was really getting at, is the amount of money spent by the parents of each of the graduating seniors. In my class for example, with approximately thirty students having attended since kindergarten and a tuition of approximately $10,000 per year (yes, even for kindergarten, and that figure has tripled in the approximately twenty years since I've graduated), that equates to approximately $3.9 million (tripled in today's dollars!!). With that kind of money, it's hard to argue against their seemingly absurd system of announcing the graduating class in ascending order by the number of years they've attended school, with the level of emphasis rising with each and every grade (and dollar, or millions, spent).

Now don't get me wrong, as mentioned before I went off on this diatribe about the elitist mentality fostered by my high school, it certainly has its attributes, chief among them a sound academic upbringing. And while I did make my share of lasting friendships (some of which I'll hopefully still have after this book), I saw my sister struggle mightily at making friends, through no fault of her own. It's particularly difficult to break through the twelve-year bond when you join in high school, as those bonds have been formed from a very young age, when kids are most impressionable. Personally speaking, I was both bullied in high school and my parents' house was robbed when I foolishly invited some of my high school "friends" over for a party. In the end, I'm glad I went to my high school, as it provided me with the academic tools necessary to succeed at the college level and beyond. More importantly, however, it made me appreciate my public grade school, public college and public law school experiences that much more, as the twelve-year members who typically go on to similar, elitist extensions of high school have little perception of reality and are generally ill-equipped to deal with the diversity and culture that exists in the real world, beyond the comforting walls of their high school.

Back to the topic which prompted the high school reminiscing, recall I said that all of my life my goal was never to have to worry about money. As a result, I've made two significant decisions over the course of my life which I've come to somewhat regret. The first was not attending UCLA for undergrad. Now recall the admonishment I just made of my high school peers for rejecting the U of I, for smaller, often academically inferior institutions which cost four or more times as much. UCLA, equal in size and on par (or perhaps superior) academically, also could have served as a gateway for my entering the entertainment industry, a goal that has always sat just beyond my horizon, and likely faded by this point in my life. But I was fortunate to be admitted to UCLA for undergrad,[5] and likely could have received in-state tuition for at least three of the four years as a result of my father living there at the time. But similar to how I followed my sister to high school, I followed her once again to the U of I.[6]

The second regret I have in life, also having to do with my career ambition of being an entertainment lawyer (think Ari

---

[5] I applied again for law school, and very likely would have gone had I been admitted, but as luck/karma would have it, I was rejected the 2nd time around.

[6] Despite my entertainment law ambitions, it is hard for me to look back on my days at the University of Illinois with anything but fondness, as I made what have thus far been my most lasting friendships in life, and undoubtedly had the best four years of my life (other than of course the four years I spent traveling the world and living abroad with my wife, and perhaps these last several years living in Colorado and exploring its beautiful mountains followed by more recently buying a 2nd home/investment property in Myrtle Beach, South Carolina and exploring its beautiful coastline and culture as well). Also, unlike most of my high school peers, after spending those years in what felt like a bubble, I actually wanted the biggest, most down to Earth college experience I could find.

22

Gold from Entourage), was when I turned down an offer to be a summer associate with a small law firm in Los Angeles which specialized in entertainment law, in favor of joining a more prestigious international law firm in Chicago. Although the pay was the same (both in terms of a summer associate salary and starting salary), in my view at the time, in the event the summer position did not matriculate into a full-time position, or in the event the full-time position was short-lived, the international Chicago firm offered a better resume builder than the smaller Los Angeles-only boutique. Moreover, the only reason I received an interview, and ultimately an offer, to join the entertainment firm in LA, was because my uncle's pizza chain was one of their clients, and my uncle was able to procure the initial interview for me. But having succeeded in law school on my own merits, I was reluctant to use nepotism to obtain employment, particularly when I received multiple offers from more prestigious, well-recognized law firms in Chicago, all on my own.

The point of these two life-altering regrets, however, is that I always swore if I was ever confronted again with the opportunity to do something different in a way that could potentially significantly increase my overall happiness in life, I would not shy away this time. For as the saying goes, you're much more likely to regret in life the things you don't do than the things you do.

Recall I said at the outset of this section that my goal in life was to never have to worry about money, within reason. That single mantra dictated my going to the U of I for undergrad, where I still took out student loans but in a far smaller amount than if I had gone to a private institution or even UCLA, and also dictated my going to the U of I College of Law, where I again took out student loans but also received a full tuition waiver by teaching a Public Speaking course to undergraduate students during my 2nd and 3rd years of law school.

For law school, my decision to attend the U of I was much easier than it was for undergrad, for unlike undergrad which I split with my parents, for law school, I had to foot the bill entirely on my own. I was accepted to at least four different law schools, one of which was Emory University in Atlanta. I recall being excited about the possibility of leaving Illinois and moving to Atlanta, that is until I saw the tuition statement of over $40,000 per year, upon which I immediately retreated to the U of I. Though the subject of a separate section discussed below, suffice to say, there was no way I was going to incur four or more times the amount of debt by going to Emory than I incurred by going to U of I for another three years, a proposition the majority of my high school peers likely wouldn't have even considered to be a factor when choosing colleges.

In fact, for better or worse, my decision to go to law school was almost entirely derived by my drive to make as much money as possible in the shortest amount of time as possible. As a senior in college who majored in Finance at the School of Business, I recall my college peers all applying for jobs with the "Big Five" (Arthur Andersen, Accenture, KPMG, PWC and E&Y). Starting salaries were around $50,000 at the time, a large sum of money for a twenty-two-year-old kid fresh out of college with no real work experience, but not enough to make me commit to a profession that frankly bored me.

Rather, by contrast, I knew that starting salaries at major law firms were $125,000 (a number that would increase to $145,000 and then again to $160,000 by the time I graduated law school three years later). Historically, I also knew that the U of I College of Law placed, on average, the top 25% of its students at big law firms in Chicago. Thus, I knew that if I could finish in the top 25% of my class, I would have a very good chance at doubling or tripling my starting salary than were I to take a finance job like most of my college peers. Moreover, if I stayed at the U of I for law school, not only would I get in-state tuition (approximately ⅓ or ¼ the price of out of state or private school tuition), I also knew there was a good chance I would be able to teach an undergraduate course my 2nd and 3rd years of law school, which would be akin to receiving free tuition for those two years.[7]

So in the end, my decision to attend the U of I for law school was a fairly easy one, though nevertheless for a kid that grew up in the heart of Chicago, the thought of living in a small town in rural Illinois for another three years, was not an ideal situation for me. But notwithstanding, I saw it as a means to an end.

When I finally told my mom and stepdad that I had decided to stay at the U of I for law school, I recall explaining my reasoning that, if I studied hard, something I rarely if ever did while in undergrad, I was confident I could place myself in the top 25% (or better) of my class after my 1L year. For those that are unfamiliar, the ability to procure a job with a top-tier law firm is almost entirely based on your 1st year ("1L") grades. For that leads to a summer associate

---

[7] On top of this, the cost of living in Champaign, Illinois was significantly cheaper than the cost of living in cities of other schools I was considering, such as Chicago, Atlanta or St. Louis. And as an added incentive, during my 1st year of law school, the Chicago Bears played at the University of Illinois while they were remodeling Soldier Field, a fact which unbeknownst to me at the time would result in my getting off the waiting list for season tickets in Chicago and ultimately getting season tickets for life. Finally, as a season ticket holder of the Fighting Illini basketball team, where the seating arrangement priority is based on a combination of the number of years you've attended the University of Illinois and the number of years you've had season tickets, I knew I would have first row floor seats by my 2nd and 3rd years of law school since I had been getting season tickets beginning my freshman year of college. Coincidentally, the Fighting Illini, with Deron Williams, Dee Brown and Luther Head, went to the National Championship game my 3rd year of law school, their only appearance in school history. I indeed had first row floor seats that entire season, and was literally on SportsCenter almost nightly.

position after your 2L year, which ultimately leads to a full-time position after graduating law school.

I was very fortunate to go to (and graduate from) law school right before the Great Recession of 2006-2007.[8] As described above, at the time, graduating near the top of your class at a top 25 law school could almost guarantee you would land a big firm job with a big firm salary. Combined with my sparkling personality and impeccable interview skills, I knew if I could get the grades, the job was basically mine for the taking.

My parents on the other hand, and my stepdad in particular, tried to keep me grounded so as to guard against any potential disappointment upon my graduation from law school. But in my view, sticking around the U of I for law school was solely a strategic and economic decision. Anything short of procuring a big firm job would have been a major disappointment. In reality, as my stepdad liked to say, even if I didn't land a top-tier job with a starting salary of $125,000 (eventually $160,000), I would likely still get a job paying $80,000-100,000, almost double that which I would have made had I taken a finance job like most of my college peers right out of college. In my view, however, that would have meant I had failed in law school. To that end, for the first time in my life, I put every ounce of effort into studying and succeeding during my first year of law school.

---

[8] Conversely, as discussed further below, I was unfortunate in that I bought a condo in Chicago right before the housing collapse, which ultimately cost me about $30,000. But if I had to choose between graduating before the recession when jobs were plentiful but the housing market was inflated and graduating after the recession when jobs were scarce but housing was cheap, I'd choose the former every time, as I likely wouldn't have been able to even afford a condo had I found myself in the latter scenario. Moreover, I likely wouldn't have even been able to get into the University of Illinois College of Law had I applied a few years later, as applications skyrocketed following the recession.

Law school is a strange beast unlike any other place for professional advancement. In law school, your ability to succeed has much more to do with your willingness to work hard than with your innate intelligence. Whereas in undergrad, many students are able to get away with missing class, skipping the assignments, and then teaching themselves the material days or even hours before the exam, in law school, with rare exception, if you don't go to class and keep up with the material, you won't do well on the exams. And in a format where 100% of your grade often depends on a single exam at the end of the semester (particularly in your first year), that is often the difference between succeeding and failing.

I have often categorized successful students (or people) into three types. The first type are those that I described above, that is, people who are so innately intelligent that they don't need to go to class nor keep up with the material, but rather, can simply teach themselves the material days or even hours before, and still do very well on the exam. Everyone knows someone like this, and we all hate them.

The second type of successful people are at the opposite end of the spectrum; people who are not that innately intelligent, but simply study harder and work harder than their peers, and consequently do well in school and in life. Everyone knows someone like this as well, and though we still may not like them, we at least have to respect them, for they make the most of their natural, if not limited, abilities.

The third type of successful people in life are people who are both innately intelligent but also work very hard. This is the category that I fall into. On standardized tests, I've always fallen into the 90-95th percentile or so, but I've never been able to consistently crack the 95th-99th percentile. However, when it comes to exams which occur in the context of classes, because they allow me to utilize my strong work ethic, I've consistently been able to propel myself into the

95th-99th percentile. For this reason, I knew I would do well in law school.

For anyone who knows me, the one ace in the hole that I've always seemed to possess which has been unmatched by anyone I've ever met, is my ability to burn the candle at both ends. In other words, I've always had the ability to stay out partying until the wee hours of the morning, and still be a productive member of society the next day. Whether it was in college, law school, or even the working world, for whatever reason, I'm able to function on very little sleep (though often lots of coffee), and so law school, which as described above, the success of which largely depends on your level of self-motivation, really suited me well. In fact, I recall one semester I had a 24-hour take-home final exam. Pickup was at 8 am. I ended up staying out all night the night before (even "sleeping" out), and picked up the exam on my way home. I stayed up eighteen straight hours to finish the exam, and received an A. In my view, there's nothing that a large coffee and a sausage, egg and cheese bagel sandwich from Dunkin Donuts can't cure. After all, "America Runs on Dunkin."[9]

Another advantage I think I had over my peers in law school was that, by staying in Champaign, IL for law school, I was not distracted by the endless possibilities of a big city, nor did I need to endure any acclimatization process to Champaign, IL. Rather, I knew where everything I needed was, and my sole focus my first year of law school was getting the best grades possible. Similar to how I was amazed by students who scored extremely high on their LSATs but then didn't put in the effort required to do well in law school, I was equally amazed by the number of students in law school who appeared to be there to make friends, have fun, or

---

[9] Ironically, nowadays and as explained further below, the more apt expression is "America runs on consumer debt."

do anything other than succeed in law school. In fact, the single largest student activity at the College of Law was a weekly Wednesday night activity called Beer League Darts, where approximately 30% of the law school (more than any law school journal or other educational activity) gathered for cheap beer and competitive (or non-competitive) darts. Although I admittedly won the league my 1L year (thanks to four years of being in a fraternity at the largest Greek system in the country, I tend to dominate bar games ☺), I often showed up just before our match and left right after, and rarely stuck around to get drunk like the majority of my peers.

Law school is like a marathon, a test of endurance, not speed. Like life, there are very few short cuts, and only those who are able to stick to the daily regime of attending class and reading the material, are likely to succeed. I am still amazed by the number of classmates I knew who scored much better than me on the LSAT (and likely the ACT/SAT before that), but fared much worse than me in law school. Perhaps the hardest part about law school is the self-discipline required to do well. With a typical class schedule of only fifteen hours per week, it is very easy to simply attend class and spend your remaining time working out, watching TV, goofing around, or doing whatever else it is that you like to do. But as someone wise told me very early on, for every hour you're in class, you should be spending two hours reading the material and preparing an outline for use come final exam time. And for anyone with ambitions of working at a big firm, forty-five hours of work per week should seem like a breeze.

Moreover, the way I looked at it, if I didn't go to law school, I would have gone straight into the working world where I would have been working a minimum of forty-five hours per week, likely more. Thus, I committed myself to working at least 45 hours per week, regardless of the number of hours I was actually attending class. In the end, as expected, I did very well in law school. Because I treated it like a job, I consequently did very well on my final exams, particularly my 1st year, which is really the only year that matters if your goal is to work at a big law firm, which indeed was my goal.[10] In the end, I had approximately twenty-five on campus job interviews for a 1L summer internship, received over ten callback/in-office interviews and over five job offers, all starting at $125,000/year, which eventually would be $160,000, before I ever began my full-time employment. Of course, there was a price to pay for this type of salary, which is largely the subject of this book. But without first experiencing the woes and sorrows of big firm law, I never would have had, nor recognized, the opportunity for greener pastures.

Perhaps the most telling story about life at a big law firm came from a magazine article I read while on my way to an interview for a summer associate position with a prestigious New York firm, one of the preeminent law firms in the world and the only firm in NYC with which I interviewed. On my flight to NYC for the interview, I was reading a Vault magazine survey which often ranks the satisfaction of attorneys at large law firms in the United States. At one point, the article said something like this: "While some law firms routinely rank well in associate satisfaction, like Chicago's Firm X [where I had previously received an offer and knew I would most likely be starting my legal career, and in fact did], other firms don't fare so well. For example, if a tidal wave came through NYC and wiped out Firm Y's [the

---

[10] I also quit smoking weed for my entire first year of law school, for I didn't want anything to affect my memory when it came time for final exams. And more importantly, I didn't want to have any excuses in the event I didn't do as well my first year as I had hoped. Rather, my thinking was that if I left everything on the table, and came up short, I could live with that result. But in the event I did fall short of my expectations, I didn't want to have any excuses, or what ifs.

NYC firm that I was on my way to interview with] entire 1st year associate class, a typical partner reaction would be something like this: 'Oh my god that's terrible news. Where in the world are we going to find more 1st year associates?'" Needless to say, having very little exposure to or knowledge of the New York legal market, but knowing there were dozens if not more of blue-chip NYC firms, the fact that this article named the one firm I was on my way to interview with, did not sit well with me.

In the end, I chose to start my career at a prestigious international law firm in Chicago. I'll never forget the day I received my offer from them to join their 1st year associate class. I drove straight from Champaign, IL to Chicago (approximately two hours), picked up a bottle of champagne along the way, and surprised my parents at dinner. Recall my stepfather, though likely doing so to guard against my potential disappointment, suggested that even if I wasn't able to land a big firm job, I could still consider law school a success if I were able to get a job with a starting salary of $80,000-90,000. Needless to say, you can imagine my level of satisfaction when I surprised him in Chicago with a bottle of champagne and my $125,000 starting salary (later $160,000; prorated at the time based on a summer internship which subsequently turned into a full-time offer).

The summer I spent with my Chicago law firm in 2003 as a summer associate is one I will never forget. We were one of the last summer associate classes before the Great Recession, when everything changed for the worse (at least from the summer associate's perspective). Prior to the recession, law firms lavished their summer associates with everything imaginable to persuade them to join their ranks. I used to akin it to rushing a fraternity, only imagine the fraternity had an unlimited budget. For twelve consecutive weeks, we dined at some of the best restaurants in Chicago. In fact, in twelve weeks, I recall eating on my own dime only twice, and both were by choice, because I simply wanted a

31

Subway or Potbelly's sandwich that day. I was literally consuming 2,000 calories before 2 pm every day. In fact, in addition to running three to four miles a day after work every day (so as to avoid gaining the equivalent of the "freshman fifteen"), I recall purposely trying to avoid going home after work (I was living with my parents during that summer) because I knew my mom was preparing a five course meal every night (don't all moms like to spoil their kids with too much food?).

In any event, one of my favorite anecdotal stories from that summer came towards the end of that summer when one of my summer associate peers (there were about thirty of us at the time) sent out an email asking if any other summer associates wanted to go to lunch with him and a few attorneys (on the firm, per usual, of course). He sent the inquiry to the all summer associate distribution list which we frequently used that summer. Typically, such requests were filled within a matter of minutes (though a summer associate never went unfed if he/she so desired). In response to that particular email, however, one of my fellow summer associates responded (replying all), "Where are you going to lunch and with whom are you dining?"

This led to another associate, one of my closest friends that summer, responding (again by replying all), "Has it really come to this? Can't you just take the free meal? Does it really matter where you're going and who you're dining with? It's about the people, not the places."

Being the extrovert and antagonist that I am, I of course felt compelled to reply (all) as well. And because he was my good friend, I was able to reply "'It's about the people, not the places?' Easy for someone to say whose 'places' this week alone [it was a Friday] included Ruth's Chris, Fogo de Chao,

Smith and Wollensky and [some other equally excellent restaurant]."[11]

The culmination of this email string ended with the original author replying all again, this time saying something to the effect of "Dear Esteemed Colleagues: I cordially invite you to dine at the following establishment with myself, and the following attorneys [with links to the attorneys' intranet profiles included]. Attached please find the restaurant's menu and also reviews. Please let me know at your earliest convenience if this is something that might interest you. Kindly, [summer associate signature]."

A similar story I recall which illustrates the over-the-top nature of the summer associate experience prior to the recession occurred a couple of years later when I was a first-year associate. Now in a position to dictate which restaurants we took our summer associates to, I, along with two other first-year associates, went on a tour of the Top 5 burgers in Chicago that summer, as proclaimed by Chicago Magazine. Three of the restaurants were downtown and thus completely within reason for a summer associate lunch. The fourth was in Lakeview, about a 20-minute cab ride from downtown. With so many fabulous restaurants within walking distance of our office downtown, there was really no reason to take a cab, let alone to Lakeview, but we were on a mission, and after all, we were still in the glory days before the recession. The fifth, and final restaurant, however, was in the suburbs of Chicago, about an hour away from our office. For that day's lunch, I drove into work, parked at a garage downtown (which I charged to the firm), and we all piled into my car for

---

[11] Truth be told, though this was all done in jest and of course we were all very appreciative just to be able to dine at Chicago's best restaurants every day for twelve weeks straight, in lieu of doing real work, by the end of the summer, most of us had been to the same restaurants with the same people multiple times, and so the opportunity to dine somewhere new with someone new, was actually enticing.

the trek to the burbs. In total, our lunch took about three hours, but was by far the "cheapest" lunch of the summer as the fifth burger spot was a hole in the wall type of joint. In terms of billable hours wasted, however, it was probably the most expensive lunch we took that summer.

In the end, being a summer associate was definitely one of the best experiences of my life. We were paid a pro-rated salary of a first-year associate (approximately $2,500 per week) but only "worked" from 9-5, and two of those hours included the aforementioned daily lunch. We were also treated to a weekly special event at night, which ranged from a rooftop Cubs game, to a private dinner at the Art Institute of Chicago, to a skybox Madonna concert at the United Center, to a Lake Michigan booze cruise on the 3rd of July. It was truly an unforgettable summer. In fact, I even made sure I had a "summer associate girlfriend" that summer so as to make me look more dependable and less non-committal. Needless to say, I worked very little that summer, as did the rest of my peers. Historically (again, pre-recession), approximately 90% of summer associates get full-time offers, and so they often say the job is yours to lose. From what I heard, of the few people that didn't get offers, it was typically due to social/behavioral problems (e.g., dressing inappropriately, talking back to a partner, speaking out of turn in front of a client or judge, etc.), as opposed to work-product issues, for frankly, we didn't have enough work-product for them to judge us by.

However, unlike my summer associate stint, the life of being a real-world lawyer (in particular for two of the largest firms in the world), was not all it's cracked up to be, or even close for that matter. Although you're paid well, you work incredibly long hours (though not as many as an investment banker or private equity, from what I hear) and the work is very tedious. Despite being very excited about the opportunity to work at a big law firm, that excitement dwindled very quickly, and reality soon set in. Looking back,

I have no idea how I made it eight years at two of the biggest firms in the world. I remember when I started out my mom said she'd be impressed if I lasted three to four years (the typical turnover period for big firm lawyers, if not shorter). But as they say, the golden handcuffs are hard to walk away from, as the pay certainly affords you every amenity you could ever want in life (at least within reason). And so for eight years, I slogged along, ignorant of the infinite possibilities for happiness that lied beyond the walls of big firm law.

As a result, fast forward eight years and several large law firms later (two before I moved to Asia and several more since, the latter mostly on a part-time basis), and though I came out a little heavier with a lot less hair, I was also fortunate enough to accumulate in a short time more money than most people will accumulate in their entire life.[12] During that time, I owned a beautiful two bedroom condo in the Fulton Market District of Chicago, a CLK 430 Mercedes, and all of the toys a successful young man in Chicago could want. The two things that eluded me, however, were professional and personal happiness.

At this point in the book, you may be thinking, with so much money saved up, of course he could do anything he wanted. Consequently, you might think that the rest of this book will be inapplicable to you because you don't have

---

[12] At present, through good investing, I have enough saved up to live comfortably in a major American city (e.g., Chicago or Denver, the latter where I presently live half the year) for 10-15 years without working at all (though I would never do so), or the rest of my life in a country like Thailand or somewhere in Latin/South America (though the visa issue would likely present a problem in the event I wasn't working there, at least until I'm 50 when you can obtain a retirement visa in many countries, which I very well might do in six years' time, in particular Thailand, my favorite of the approximately 70 countries I've visited thus far).

anywhere close to that amount of savings. To that end, I offer two responses. First, yes, I am very fortunate in that I had a great upbringing (largely thanks to my mom and stepdad whom this book is dedicated to) but I also worked my ass off from the age of twenty-two to thirty-three. So I don't think I was handed anything (other than the wonderful aforementioned mom/stepdad), but rather, I worked for everything I've accomplished. Second, you don't need nearly as much money as I saved up before taking a leap of faith like I took. It just so happened that the timing worked out for me as such. But had the circumstances been different (namely meeting my now ex-wife earlier in life), I gladly would have taken my leap a few years earlier, when I had far less saved up. Moreover, however, as this book illustrates later on, no matter how much money you have saved, if you simply change your everyday spending habits and reprioritize how you spend your money (particularly on big item purchases), your savings will add up quickly, and soon enough, you too will feel comfortable enough to take the leap.

Part Three

The Convincing Yourself (aka Pulling the Trigger) Stage

I often used to joke (partially true however) that the real reason I quit my job is because I've always wanted to hike to Mt. Everest Base Camp, and it takes two weeks, without internet for most of the time. And while I could likely get two weeks off work (though that would constitute my entire vacation for the year), going two weeks without being able to check my work email would be nearly impossible (or at best, an absolute nightmare upon returning to work).

Personal Happiness

As described above, it wasn't until my father died, when I was twenty-seven, that I began to truly evaluate what's most important in life. Unfortunately, at that time, I was only two years into my legal career, and had just purchased a $380,000 condo only a few months earlier. Thus, I wasn't really in a position to dramatically change my financial lifestyle. But nevertheless, I began to view life differently, and knew something had to change for the better eventually.[1]

---

[1] Interestingly and also very importantly/aptly, I remember (how could you not) the precise moment I learned my father died. I received a call from my ex-stepmother on a weeknight while at my office in Chicago. She broke the news (he had been sick leading up to that point but also misled his family, or at least my sister and me, as to the true extent of his cancer diagnosis/prognosis). Upon hearing the news, I drafted a handwritten letter to the partner I primarily worked for (to inform him I

37

I firmly believe there are two things that can make a person happy. First, find what it is that you like to do most, and do that (we'll call this "professional happiness"). Second, as alluded to earlier, find someone you love that shares those same passions, and spend as much time with that person as possible (we'll call this "personal happiness"). At the time my father died, when I finally began to recognize these two keys to happiness, as suggested above, I was not in a position to financially forego my big firm salary in order to find something that made me happier (i.e., professional happiness). Thus, instead, I began to look for someone to share my life with in hopes of solving the personal happiness aspect to life. I figured the professional happiness could come later, after I had hopefully made a good deal of money and thus could spend some of it in further pursuit of my personal happiness.

However, just because I was finally open to the idea of finding a partner with whom to share my life, didn't mean I was willing to settle. For my entire life, I've firmly believed

---

needed a couple of weeks off to bury my father in Chicago and then fly to Los Angeles, where he was living at the time of his death, to wrap up a few of his loose ends) and went into his office to drop it off on his desk. To my surprise (or perhaps not), he was still in the office as well, finishing up work at his computer. It must have been after 7 or 8 pm. While actually an extremely nice man (rare at the types of firms I worked for; see FN 9 in this section) and frankly the best boss I've ever had, he was also on the heavier side and had several children at home. He was undoubtedly making upwards of $1 million/year and likely had been making that amount for some time. Yet he was still there (like me) after 7 or 8 pm on a weeknight (like most weeknights) working at his computer. But this wonderful man also must have been my father's age (63 at the time he died) or very close to it. And I knew right then and there that I didn't want to work at a desk doing something I didn't particularly enjoy doing, consequently keeping me from spending time with the people I loved until the day I died. As such, it was at that moment in time I knew I no longer wanted to be a partner at a law firm, a goal I had been striving for literally my entire life up to that point.

that I'd rather be single and sometimes lonely rather than be with someone who wasn't right for me. Whereas I've seen many of my friends settle for fear of being alone, for me, there are simply too many attributes in someone that I either can't live with or can't live without, to justify settling. And though I never thought about finding love before my father died, after seeing him die alone, divorced twice, I knew I'd rather try to find love than continue being oblivious to it (i.e., I figured if I was going to die alone like my father, I'd rather go down swinging rather than looking).

Prior to my father passing, I dated a myriad of women, without any real regard to finding the aforementioned attributes. Now, for the first time in my life, I went on each new date looking for my wife. Of course, as they say, when you're looking for love, you're unlikely to find it. But that didn't stop me from looking.

And boy did I look. In the six or so years before I met my (now ex) wife, I tried all sorts of ways to find love. From online dating (JDate, Match.com and eHarmony; this was before dating apps), to setups, to bars, to coffee shops, to bookstores, to chatting up girls on buses and trains, I tried them all. At one point, I even paid $2,000 to join a professional matchmaking service for busy executives, by far the worst investment of my life up to that point. Of the twenty-five or so dates I went on in a six-month period, I only found three of the girls to be attractive, and two of them I had already dated on my own volition before joining the service (shockingly, I even suspected I knew one of the girls I was being setup with based on their description, but they incorrectly assured me I was mistaken).

Based on my thirteen or so years of dating before I met my wife (from approximately eighteen to thirty-one), and in particular my six years of what I'd call serious dating (from the time my father died until I met my wife), I developed a list of attributes that I call "deal breakers" (i.e., if a girl either has a specific attribute or lacks it, I knew I couldn't spend my entire life with her; dating her for a few months/weeks or even a night was a different story:). None of these attributes are physical. Obviously, you have to be physically attracted to someone to even consider spending the rest of your life with them. Thus, all of my deal breakers are personality attributes. And significantly, all of them stem from women I've dated over the course of my life, and thus for each attribute, I have a specific anecdotal story about why a girl either had or didn't have an attribute. Remarkably, after thirteen years of searching and six years of serious searching, I found all of these attributes in my now ex-wife. And even more remarkably, the five or so most important attributes on my list, were her greatest (or strongest) attributes.[2] In fact, on our first several dates, I recall my ex-wife doing or saying several things that literally made me look up to the sky and say "am I on Candid Camera or something," for it's as if she knew exactly what to do or say that would make me happy.

Also, not surprisingly, I met my ex-wife through a blind setup by my best friend from college (in turn I set him up with his future fiancé years earlier), her client at the time. A few weeks before, he had set me up with another girl whom I found to be very unattractive. In his defense, he told me he had only seen pictures of that girl whereas "this girl" he had met in person, so he assured me of her attractiveness. Nevertheless, due to my skepticism, I showed up to our first date drunk with another date lined up for later that night. Needless to say, I never made it to that 2nd date.

For those of you interested in hearing about these attributes, along with a few of the anecdotal stories which led to their inception, here are the Top 10.

1. A willingness to try new things (whether it be a new food, new activity, new city/country, etc.). Try it and

---

[2] Ultimately, for a variety of reasons alluded to further below, my wife and I divorced, but at the time, she was the perfect match for me.

tell me you don't like it, and that's fine, I'll never ask you to try it again. But knock it before you've even tried it, and that's where you've lost me. This attribute developed when I took my law school girlfriend (a college senior at the time and also a cheerleader in the most popular sorority on campus; I recall at one time, her two roommates, also cheerleaders, were dating a future NBA and NFL player, and here I was, this short-ish, Jewish white kid dating the third roommate) home to Chicago for a weekend. She had never tried sushi, so I took her to a nice sushi restaurant in the neighborhood where I grew up. But despite my several protests, she refused to try it, and instead opted for chicken teriyaki. At that moment, I knew she was not for me (long-term at least).

2. A passion in life other than having children. Every woman, with the fortune of good health and an able/willing partner (or the resources/desire to do it alone), has the ability to bear children. But what not every woman has is a passion to do something beyond that. Whether it's with respect to your career, a hobby, or whatever, whomever I'm with needs to be passionate about what they're doing, and my ex-wife, certainly had that in spades. This attribute developed from a North Shore (North Shore refers to the north suburbs of Chicago, a largely Jewish community much like Long Island in New York)[3] girl I dated right after I began my legal career.

---

[3] Not surprisingly, I likely didn't find my ex-wife until the age of thirty-one because the majority of girls I dated were from the North Shore, which like Long Island girls, tend to be very "jappy" (for those not in the know, a "JAP" is a Jewish American Princess, in other words, a very spoiled person with little sense of reality). My ex-wife, on the other hand, was from Columbus, Ohio, so she was anything but jappy.

She had been a teacher at a Jewish day school in Michigan where she was engaged to be married. But she left her fiancé and returned to Chicago. When we met, she was unemployed but said she was looking for a teaching job in Chicago. Because it was the middle of the school year, she proclaimed teaching jobs were hard to come by. Be that as it may, she remained unemployed for the entire time we were dating (approximately nine months). One day, she called me at work, in the middle of the day, told me she was at Target doing some shopping and asked if I needed anything. I replied, "yes, I need you to find a job." In my view, although she was a teacher by trade, after nine months of being unemployed, she should have taken a job in retail or at a local restaurant or something else. Why she thought she had earned the right to retire at the age of twenty-five was beyond me. Even more disturbing was that her parents paid her mortgage on a beautiful condo in downtown Chicago, which gave her even less of an incentive to work. In the end, I simply began to devalue her opinion.

We used to fight about everything (which to some degree was fun and much better than being a "yes, ma'am" type of girl—i.e., a girl who says yes to everything you propose and has no opinion of her own, another deal breaker of mine), but eventually, when we began fighting about what restaurant we would eat dinner at or what movie we would go to, my response would be "well you can go to that restaurant and movie tomorrow while I'm working." Once I considered her time to be less valuable than mine, I knew it was time to move on.

3. A related, but slightly different attribute, is a hard worker. I don't do laziness, and fortunately neither did my ex-wife. While some women (I've dated a few) can sleep away their Saturday or even their vacation, my

ex-wife, like me, would be up at the crack of dawn and wouldn't rest until the clock struck midnight, so to speak. Related to this is also the desire to work out and stay in shape. Unless you're one of those rare birds (like my sister) who looks fabulous but stays in shape doing yoga and somehow manages to get in 10,000 steps per day, I need to be with someone who likes to stay active and fit. For as evidenced by my 1st and 6th attributes, I simply can't afford not to.

4. This next attribute is where I've lost many women over my life. Every girl likes a five-star hotel (e.g., Four Seasons, Ritz-Carlton, etc.). Who doesn't? I do too (particularly when I'm not paying). But what I had been looking for, and found in my ex-wife, is someone who's also willing to sleep in the jungle, climb a mountain, sleep in tents, go days or maybe even weeks without showering if the circumstances call for it, etc. My ex-wife was the most adventurous person I know, male or female, next to me of course:). This attribute arose when I asked a girl I was dating if she wanted to take a trip to Brazil with me, all expenses paid. Her response was "Wow, sounds amazing. What will we do?"

To which I responded, "Well, I'm thinking of three nights in Rio de Janeiro, a week at the beaches and then three nights in the Amazon."

She responded, "Sounds awesome, but what's the Amazon going to be like? Will there be showers, electricity, etc.?"

I responded, "It's the Amazon. Obviously it's going to be the worst experience of your life [I knew she was, relatively speaking, high-maintenance]. But also will you come back 10 times of a better human being for having seen things that you can only imagine which will also make you appreciate everything you have in life that much more? Yes that will happen for you too."

After pondering momentarily, she replied that she was in for the trip generally but out for the Amazon, to which I replied (at least in my mind), that I was out on her. Ultimately, I ended up going to Brazil with a different good friend from high school, Dutch style, and then went back with my ex-wife years later, including to the Amazon.

5. A seemingly simple attribute but one that's surprisingly difficult to find is someone who has both a good set of friends of their own, and is also easily able to assimilate with yours. Technically these are two different attributes but my ex-wife had them both. And regarding the latter, in my view, the key is being able to leave your significant other with your friends for an extended period of time if needed, and knowing that she'll be fine fending for herself. Years ago, for example, my ex-wife and I went to Florida with my best girlfriends from college, and when I left her for the day to golf with my good buddy (one of their husbands), she stayed with my friends, and rightly so, I knew she would fit right in, which of course she did.

6. Although related to #1, this attribute is so important that it warrants a separate category all by itself. A love of food. Food is one of, if not my greatest, passions in life. And when I say a love of food, I'm talking about all kinds of food. From 5-star restaurants like Alinea (in Chicago) to dive biker bars like Kuma's Corner (also Chicago) to greasy spoons like In-N-Out to the abundance of street food we ate in Thailand and all throughout Asia, my ex-wife, like me, liked it all. The fact that she had her own food blog said it all. And similar to my first attribute, the love of my life has to be open to eating all types of food, whether an exotic vegetable, exotic meat, or exotic animal body part. For example, on our Round the World ("RTW" 2.0), we had dog in Vietnam (called thit cho), snake in

44

Indonesia, live octopus in South Korea, and who knows what during our five weeks in China where almost every meal consisted of going into a crowded restaurant and pointing at what looked good, which was always the case, literally every single time (it was often frog, fyi). The point is, if it's popular in a particular country/region then it's seemingly delicious, and just because some cultures decided to domesticate a certain animal (e.g., the dog in Western cultures), other cultures (e.g., Hindus) have decided that the cow (an animal that most other cultures/countries eat routinely) is the sacred, "off limits," animal. Or for Jewish people, pork, which most chefs (and myself, despite being Jewish) would likely say is their first choice of meat to work/cook with.[4]

7. Another seemingly simple attribute but one that's surprisingly hard to find, is tolerant of all cultures, races, ethnicities, and religions, which more recently, includes not being on either end of the politically extreme spectrum (be it too far left or right).[5] A

---

[4] As another aside/illustrative point, on my 1st date with my ex-wife (the blind setup by my best friend, recall), she broke out a color-coded spreadsheet with all the Chicago restaurants that she a) wanted to try; b) had already tried; and c) needed to investigate further. It was literally at that moment in time when I knew I would marry her (and also asked if I was on Candid Camera).

[5] Without getting too political, I used to be a liberal Democrat but now I'm more of a socialist libertarian (i.e., let's try to help as many people as we can and then get out of our way and let everyone do whatever makes them happy in this short life we're given so long as they don't hurt other people intentionally—e.g., if people want to smoke weed in their home or even cigarettes at a restaurant/bar just let them and you don't have to go to their home or patronize/work at that restaurant). As a result, I have equal disdain for both far right Republicans and far left liberals/Democrats, though in my personal observations/experience, the far left tend to have more disdain for the far right than vice versa which makes them the worser of two evils, again in my personal opinion.

Particularly considering the far left, again very generally speaking and just based on my personal observations/experience, tend to be better off economically (and generally afforded more opportunities in life) than the far right, my personal disdain is more recently geared towards the far left. This is particularly so since the far left, on the whole, often have greater ability to travel and visit the places where the far right tend to live (e.g. Alabama, Mississippi), but instead choose not to (rather choosing to stay in their liberal bubble or only visiting other liberal places with like-minded people—e.g., Hawaii, Napa Valley, Paris) but nevertheless judge and look down upon the far right. I'm also a firm believer that if you care about something in life enough you do it, and if not, you make an excuse. And for my entire existence liberals have purported to care about things like gun violence, economic inequality, and abortion (issues I care deeply about) yet have done literally nothing or at best very little to actually solve them. Instead, for literally decades, they just blame the "other side." And while I was once naïve enough to believe that, after publishing a 60-page article in law school about how the President has the power (be it through Executive Order or the Spending Clause) to force states to comport to his or her agenda (essentially overruling the Constitution) under the guise of a national emergency (*see* 9-11 directly after which Muslin-Americans lost many of their constitutional rights and/*or* Covid-19 where we put 40 million, mostly young, healthy Americans out of work against their will for the first time since the military draft, a fact mentioned by our courts in support of a ruling striking down one of the lockdown orders as being unconstitutional), I'm no longer so obtuse. Look no further than my own city, Chicago, the gun capital of the developed world. For 50 years we've led the country in gun violence and we know the exact neighborhood, and literally street(s), where it happens. Yet for 50 years we've done nothing to solve it, even with a black mayor and black President. The only logical conclusion one can reach based on those facts is not only don't we/they care about it enough, but sadly, they actually want it to continue. For ultimately it means the rich stay rich and the poor stay poor (and also related population control), which is literally the only thing Democrats and Republicans agree on and also the reason why the Democratic party literally rigged the election against the one guy who actually wanted to solve this country's aforementioned obvious problems (Bernie Sanders, the guy I would have voted for if given the opportunity/his own party didn't literally rig the election against him once they realized that unlike them, he might actually help poor people; a fact which led to the resignation of the head of the Democratic National Committee after leaked emails to that effect were discovered). But I common attribute that my ex-wife and I both share that I think helped define who we are and which served us well on our across the globe journey, is that we both went to a combination of public and private school (albeit at different points in our lives; she went to private grade school and public high school whereas I did the opposite). And as described above, while the private schooling certainly helped shape our professional success, it's the public schooling that I think helped shape who we really are. Though not a dating story, I recall one event from college which merits discussion here.

Shortly after arriving at college my freshman year, I joined a predominantly Jewish fraternity made up primarily of guys from the North Shore of Chicago (my reasons for joining it had nothing to do with being Jewish but rather my sister just happened to be dating a guy in that fraternity when I came to visit her my senior year and so they rushed me hard and "sucked me in"). One weekend, my friend from grade school who's Hispanic and also went to the U of I, came over to my fraternity to visit. As we were walking through the

---

digress and this will likely be discussed ad nauseum in my next book discussing the problems that American society suffers from (e.g., politics and socio-economic issues) which literally no other country in the world tolerates or would tolerate (see the aforementioned gun violence and also the fact that five Americans, who not coincidentally generally happen to be the five biggest employers in the U.S.—Bill Gates, Mark Zuckerberg, Elon Musk and Jeff Bezos to name four of them—have the same combined wealth as the bottom 50% of the U.S.; think about that staggering fact for a minute and how if changed it would drastically improve the lives of literally tens if not hundreds of millions of Americans; contrast that with one of Joe Biden's first acts/orders as President of the U.S., a transgender military bill which putting aside your thoughts on that issue likely improved the lives of only a handful of Americans).

hallways, I'll never forget the looks on the faces of my fraternity brothers some of whom legitimately thought he was robbing our house. In their defense, they very likely may have never seen a Hispanic person before. Needless to say, this was a quality that I would not tolerate in my soul mate.

8. Knowing the value of a dollar (or a thousand). As evidenced by the comprehensive wedding section discussed further below, my ex-wife was the most practical woman I'd ever met when it comes to money. While most women want fancy rings, big weddings, pretty flowers, expensive clothes, etc., my ex-wife like me, at least at the time I met her (more on that below), wanted experiences in life. For as the expression goes, experiences are the most valuable things you can buy in life. With my ex-wife, however, I knew I'd never need to worry about spending money on frivolous things you don't really need in life, a problem I saw my father struggle with his entire life. Moreover, though I fully intended to, I knew I never really needed to "take care" of my ex-wife, as she was fully capable of taking care of herself, as evidenced by her one-off jobs (selling paintings, babysitting, numerous websites she's developed and now thriving business which is one of the many reasons we're now divorced), or just her general cognizance of the value of a dollar (e.g., using coupons, selling clothes she didn't need, etc.).

9. Intelligence: Truth be told, this is not on my "must have" list but my ex-wife was so intelligent that I just had to put it on this list. And when I say intelligent, I'm not talking about book smart. I'm book smart (or one would hope so after seven years of post-high school education). But my ex-wife was practical smart. Whether it's electronics, the internet, social media, or anything that anyone would want to use on an everyday basis, she could literally do in a matter of minutes or

hours what would take me days or weeks, assuming I could do it at all. From her Valentine's Day video she made for me, to her paintings, to the honeyfund website she created which helped pay for our around the world trip before our move to Thailand (or at least gave people the perception that their wedding gift helped pay for our trip; more on that below) and beyond, my ex-wife is one of the most practically intelligent people I know. As I used to like to put it, when we were together, I may have been the one who came up with the idea, but she was typically the one who went out and actually made it a reality/implemented it.

10. Last, but certainly not least and arguably most important of all, was her loyalty, at least until the months leading up to our divorce for which her change of heart was likely warranted. But prior to that, I had never met anyone more loyal than my ex-wife. When we were dating/married, I knew in my heart of hearts that there was nothing she wouldn't do for me, and I for her. Whether it was taking our 120-hour online Teaching English in a Foreign Language ("TEFL") course (shhh, don't tell anyone), planning our RTW, making my lunches, or just being there one of the many times I needed to vent, she was the most loyal person I've ever known, and for that attribute alone, I will be forever grateful and indebted to her.

So that's it. My ex-wife, in a nutshell. Pretty remarkable if you ask me. But then again, I'd hope so since I married her. And while our paths, as explained further below, may have led us down different roads later in life, hopefully this paints a little better of a picture for you about my ex-wife, and why for a seven-year period (but more like 25-30 years for the typical American couple, as also explained further below), she was the love of my life. And more importantly, hopefully this illustrates how once I was finally able to achieve the

49

"personal happiness" I had so long been striving for, I could finally turn my attention to achieving the 2nd component to a happy life, "professional happiness."

And in case any of you were interested in hearing the other endless number of attributes that made my ex-wife such a perfect fit for me, at least at the time, here are a few more, in no particular order: a good sense of humor, a stylish dresser, able to party hard but not harder than me, and accepts me for who I am without trying to change me (faults and all, of which there are many, like lack of brevity).

Professional Happiness

For eight years, I practiced law at two of the largest firms in the world, first in Chicago for six years, then in New York for two. I started out as a general commercial litigator in one of Chicago's preeminent commercial litigation practices. After two years of mostly reviewing documents (aka document review), I decided I needed to gain more actual legal experience, and realized that likely wasn't going to happen at my firm, as commercial litigation was their bread and butter practice, and Chicago was their largest office, so basically I was the lowest man on the totem pole.

Despite my initial dislike of big firm law, I wasn't ready to move to a smaller firm, as I had worked too hard in law school to give up so early. So instead I decided to look at large law firms with smaller Chicago offices, and also smaller practices. I eventually narrowed it down to two firms, both in Chicago but both with smaller offices than my original firm. The offer I ended up taking was with an up-and-coming insurance recovery practice. The offer I turned down was in a small but very reputable construction litigation practice. Although I knew very little about either niche practice, I eventually chose the insurance practice, namely after an associate in the construction litigation practice essentially told me it was a sweat shop.[6] And also after the head partner in that practice could only meet with me at 6 am for a breakfast meeting (note to future hiring partners--even if you don't have the time to meet with potential candidates during regular business hours, make the time, or just don't bother meeting them).

The insurance recovery (aka insurance coverage) practice that I joined is one of the best in the world.[7] There are numerous types of insurance coverage, but the two biggest types are called directors' and officers' liability coverage (aka D&O insurance) and commercial general liability (aka CGL) insurance. The former provides insurance for corporations (and also for its directors and officers) for decisions made by the company and/or its directors and officers that are essentially within the business judgment rule but ultimately end up costing the company millions (or billions) of dollars. For the non-lawyers out there, the business judgment rule is a rule of law that says so long as a company (and its directors and officers) act with the best interests of the company and its shareholders (and not in the best interests of the individual directors and officers) in mind, they will not be legally liable for any costs which result from poor decision-making. Frankly, without this rule, nobody would ever serve as an officer or director of a corporation for fear of being personally responsible for a business decision that went south.

---

[6] In truth, I think he may have just told me that so that he could avoid the competition for work which may have arisen had I joined his group, but either way, after hearing those remarks, it was enough to dissuade me from joining.

[7] Admittedly, and as I was told by the woman I've been recently dating, the next couple of pages which discuss the intricacies of my legal profession are very nuanced and might be perceived as boring by some. Rather than omitting them, I've kept them in but feel free to skip a couple of pages if you find yourself bored too.

Classic examples of D&O insurance involve shareholder lawsuits, class actions by consumers, breach of contract lawsuits brought by other companies, and even government investigations or lawsuits. Any of the aforementioned activities typically cost companies hundreds of millions of dollars, which is why they buy insurance to protect themselves against such activity. A typical D&O policy can provide anywhere from $1 million to hundreds of millions of dollars in insurance. The insurance provides protection against defense costs incurred by the company (the Insured) as a result of a covered Claim (e.g., a lawsuit or government investigation), and also against any judgments (aka verdicts) against the company, any settlements made by it, or even any fines levied by the government.

Typically, when a company tenders a Claim to an insurance company and asks them to pay their defense costs, judgments/settlements or fines, the insurance company responds by saying the Insured acted outside the scope of the business judgment rule (i.e., its directors and officers either broke the law and/or acted in their own best interests rather than in the best interest of the company). The Insured typically responds by saying that until there has been an "adjudication of fraud" (i.e., a finding of guilt by a jury), the insurer must pay. For this reason, insureds often settle Claims well before they ever advance to the jury stage for fear of an adverse ruling which would result in the loss of insurance coverage. Ultimately, the Insured and Insurer typically settle and agree on a portion of the defense costs/judgment/settlement that the insurer will pay. On a typical policy with $100 million in limits, an insurer might pay $50-75 million while the insured funds the rest. There are several default legal rules which highly favor the insured (e.g., if the insurance policy language is ambiguous, the language must be read in favor of the insured under the presumption that the insurance company drafted the ambiguous language; policy exclusions are interpreted narrowly; and grants of coverage are interpreted broadly), which make this a lucrative profession if you're a good insurance coverage lawyer. As a partner I worked with used to say, "Insurance is cheap. Insurance coverage, however, is not."

During my time at my second firm, I worked on numerous D&O claims, ranging from lawsuits involving alleged horse breeding schemes, to lawsuits involving allegedly poor mortgage loan practices, to numerous claims involving government investigations into certain corporate governance issues. The mortgage loan case I worked on spanned almost a decade and at one point I was told it was the largest case in the U.S. (at any law firm) with the largest legal budget (our client was spending millions of dollars per month in legal fees) and the largest amount at stake (approximately one billion dollars). During that time I was managing over fifty contract attorneys at an offsite office in Chicago over the course of several or more years. Suffice to say, it was a grind but very lucrative for all the lawyers involved.

In truth, at times, I questioned whether our client had acted improperly but because of the pro-insured default rules, and because of the wealth of knowledge and experience held by my colleagues, our clients often obtained very favorable results. In fact, in terms of return on investment, few (if any) legal practices can offer as much as insurance coverage lawyers. In a typical case for example, a client might incur a few hundred thousand dollars in legal fees (or even a few million if the case is huge) but might be able to obtain upwards of $50-100 million worth of insurance coverage (or more). For this reason, more and more insurance coverage lawyers are seeking contingency fee arrangements rather than fixed fee payments (e.g., arrangements where the lawyer receives 10-30% of whatever amount they are able to obtain from the insurance company, rather than a flat fee based on the number of hours worked).[8]

The second most popular type of insurance coverage is called CGL insurance. This insurance provides protection for companies against Claims which result in the loss of substantial property for a company. For example, companies with properties in areas affected by natural disasters (e.g., hurricanes, tornadoes, earthquakes, etc.), or companies involved with a major accident (e.g., a Gulf oil spill or manufacturing plant explosion). Sometimes a company may literally lose the property and seek recovery for its value. Other times, the company may simply be out of business for an extended period of time (e.g., a hotel, a manufacturing plant) and seek recovery for the loss caused by the business interruption (aka a business interruption claim). Like D&O claims, these claims can often be worth hundreds of millions of dollars. Also like D&O claims, insurers often (or always) push back and argue that a certain claim is not covered because it doesn't fall within the scope of coverage or is excluded by a policy provision (e.g., they might argue that their policy only provides coverage for certain types of natural disasters, or that the alleged accident was really the result of negligence or even purposeful behavior). Again, like D&O insurance, the insured and insurer often settle their dispute, with the result being that the insurance company agrees to pay a certain, often substantial, portion of the insured's property damage/loss.

Like D&O insurance, in my six years at my second law firm, I worked on many types of CGL claims, from claims involving Gulf oil spills, to claims stemming from Hurricane Katrina in New Orleans and Hurricane Sandy in NYC, to

---

[8] Not surprisingly, only the partners who negotiate these contingency fee arrangements reap the rewards of them. The associates, who often do the bulk of the work leading up to the favorable results obtained from the insurance company, are always paid on a salary basis.

claims stemming from the wildfires in California. In my experience, CGL claims often involved less egregious alleged behavior by the insureds than D&O claims, but often received similarly favorable results, mostly due to the pro-insured laws and also superior lawyering by my colleagues.

In addition to D&O and CGL claims, I also worked on crime and fidelity bond claims, claims involving defamation and patent/trademark infringement, and my personal favorite, even a kidnap and ransom claim (i.e., where a company purchases insurance in the event one of its executives or officers is kidnapped; in my case, the executive was actually just detained by local authorities in a foreign country for an extended period of time, but we argued the claim was covered by the company's kidnap and ransom policy in part because it was highly publicized and led to considerable loss of business by our client which is ultimately the purpose of the insurance coverage).

As interesting as I've made (or attempted to make) my former practice out to be, in reality, it's just like any other practice at a major law firm. In other words, I sat at a computer for 10-12 hours a day, mostly writing briefs that the partners would eventually edit (or often re-write completely) and sometimes even argue in court (most often without my being there). On a good day, I might have three or more conference calls for an hour or so at a time. On a bad (which seemed more abundant than good) day, however, I would have three or more conference calls but still be responsible for churning out a brief, coverage letter, or some other writing that required my undivided attention, which could typically only be obtained before 9 am or after 6 pm. And on every day, without fail, I would receive anywhere from 10-100 emails, most of which I was expected to respond to within an hour, or at worst by the end of the day.[9] I did this for eight years. And I was paid very handsomely for it. But eventually, the daily grind got to me and I realized there had to be more to life than this.

After about three years at my second firm and five of years of big law total, I started thinking about doing something different. By that time, I had compiled enough savings (approximately $400,000) not to have to worry about money for a long time (on average, I was spending approximately $60,000/year living in Chicago so 400K in savings would have lasted me about 6-7 years if I was unemployed the entire time, which of course never would have happened given my generally hard-working nature). Having already practiced law at two of the biggest firms in the world, I knew I didn't want to move to another big firm. And moving to a smaller firm or an in-house position would have meant a substantial pay cut, all so that I could remain doing

---

[9] At one point, I recall having to turn on my Out of Office reply (back when those were a thing) and state "I'm in the office but working diligently on another matter. Unless your inquiry is urgent, I will respond at my earliest opportunity but a later time." Needless to say, this did not sit well with one of the partners I worked with, but with the dozens or more emails a day I was receiving at the time, I really didn't have any other choice if I also wanted/was expected to produce "substantive work." By way of example, I recall during one of my annual reviews, a partner telling me "You're a really hard worker and everyone likes you here, but frankly, I just don't think you're smart enough to be here." Considering that partner went to Stanford undergrad and law (not uncommon for the caliber of firm I worked for, though as discussed further below, my peers often regretted going to such high-cost schools when they realized they ultimately made the same amount as someone like me who went to a state school for seven years), I certainly wasn't as "smart" as him, but also needless to say, that was one of the several moments in my life where I knew I wasn't cut out for the "golden handcuffs" partnership track. But I plugged away for several or more years anyways, being the diligent, hard-working person I am. As for my response to that partner, I simply said "I'll try to work on that before next year's review☺"

something that I didn't even enjoy to begin with. So instead, I thought of putting my hard-earned money to better use by traveling the world. I recall asking several of my friends if they might be interested in such a trip, but there were no takers (ironically, one of my best friends and roommate at the time eventually ended up taking his own RTW a couple of years later and provided inspiration for my own RTW shortly after his).

Then, I met my future (now ex) wife, and everything changed. I remember after we had been dating only a few weeks, I told her I was generally unhappy with my job, and had been looking to make a change for some time. In fact, I was finally at the point where I felt comfortable enough to resign and take the leap of faith. But as I stated earlier, in my view, there are two kinds of happiness in life: personal happiness and professional happiness. At the time I met her, I had neither. But after only a few weeks of dating, I knew she might be the key to my finding personal happiness, so I couldn't risk walking away from that without further exploration. Nevertheless, I was still unhappy with my job, and so instead of traveling the world, I floated the idea of moving to New York together (literally after we had been dating only a few months), and she was up for it.

The idea was that I would ask my law firm to transfer me to their NYC office (since I had been practicing law for seven consecutive years, I could apply for reciprocity to the New York bar, which meant I only had to pay a fee instead of taking their bar exam, and my law firm even paid the fee). Of course, as described above, this was all before Covid-19 made remote working more palatable, even for big companies/law firms. While I would still be working for the same firm and practicing the same type of law, at least I would be in NYC, a city I always wanted to live in. So that would be new and exciting, at least for a little while. But rest assured, when I broached the idea of moving to New York with my then girlfriend/future wife, I told her it would likely only be a temporary move (maybe a year or two), as I still had the urge to travel the world. To my surprising delight, she was game. For everything.

I remember the day I knew that moving to New York could be a real possibility for me and my ex-wife. After a few weeks of dating, she had a trip planned to NYC to visit some of her friends from college. She went to the University of Maryland for college, and consequently, she told me that most of her friends lived in New York. In my mind, "most" meant a few or maybe four or five. So imagine my surprise when I'm sitting at home in Chicago on a Saturday night pregaming with my buddies and I see her tagged in a post on Facebook (Instagram wasn't a thing yet lol) with a "few" of her friends. In her case, a few meant 15-20. Literally, the post she was tagged in consisted of 15-20 mostly attractive twenty-four-year-old girls, with no dudes. Not a single one. Being the single thirty-three year old guy that I was, I immediately thought to myself "Ok, I could probably move to NYC and be friends with these girls too."[10] And on top of her friends, she also had a bunch of family in NYC, including two sets of aunts and uncles, another uncle, several cousins and grandparents. I had no family and only a few friends in New York.

So after only a few weeks of dating, I officially asked my law firm to transfer me to their NYC office. In addition to using the fact that I was in the process of getting licensed to practice in New York, I was able to use my ex-wife's

---

[10] In reality, I had wanted to move to NYC on my own a couple of years before I ever met my ex-wife. But my biggest fear (and reason for not doing so), was that I only knew 4-5 people in NYC, whereas I knew hundreds of people in Chicago. In Chicago, my biggest annoyance was doing the same thing over and over again on a regular basis (e.g., same bars, same group of friends, etc.), but my fear in moving to NYC was that I wouldn't have any friends to go to the bars (or do anything) with. Meeting my ex-wife changed all of this.

connections as a way to convince them of the seriousness of my interest in moving there. To my dismay, after making my initial request, I didn't hear back from anyone at my firm for about two months. Then, on a late Friday afternoon one day, the partner I worked most closely with (and who put in the request on my behalf; the same partner I wrote the letter to about my dad's death years earlier), called me into his office and told me that my request had been granted. And even more shocking, I would begin working there at the beginning of the New Year, a mere six weeks away. Though I would have loved to tell her this news in person, my ex-wife was actually out of town on business in Houston when I got the news. So instead I had to call her and tell her over the phone that in six weeks' time, we would be moving to the Big Apple.

Needless to say, the next six weeks were a whirlwind. Between renting out my condo and her apartment, the latter of which proved to be a nightmare due to some roommate issues which required my legal expertise, selling my car, finding a place to live in Manhattan[11] and saying goodbye to

---

[11] Finding a place to live in Manhattan provided its own special story. I recall when I first told my ex-wife we were moving to NYC, she said we'd need to visit there at least three times before finding a place to live: first to see if we "get along" in NYC, second to see what neighborhood we liked best, and third to find a specific place. I, of course, laughed and could only respond with "Honey, with respect to your first point, remember when we talked about moving to NYC and I told you that once I ask my firm to move me there, if they say yes, there's no turning back. Well, I'm going now with or without you, so hopefully we get along there." In the end, we didn't end up visiting NYC even once before ultimately moving there, mainly because we got very lucky and were able to sublet from a friend of a friend who was moving in with her boyfriend (now husband). For those that don't know, finding a place to live in Manhattan typically requires paying a broker fee equal to one month's rent. And with our rent being almost $3,000/month, it was a huge relief to avoid that fee.

our friends and family in Chicago, it was probably the fastest six weeks of my life to date.

Living in NYC was a dream come true. Definitely the best two years of my professional life at that point in time, and maybe the best two years of my life period up to that point, though college will always be hard to beat, especially my six months "studying" abroad in Australia. Between a new city, new apartment, new restaurants, new bars, new friends, and new family, it was truly a blessing. One of my favorite memories was our weekly Wednesday night dates, where for the first few months, we would check out a new neighborhood and a new restaurant within that neighborhood. One of the best things about living in NYC is the ease of getting around via the subway, whereas in Chicago you really need to drive to check out certain different neighborhoods. And even better, being the functioning alcoholics that my ex-wife and I were (joking, sort of), every Wednesday, she would meet me at the train station near my office around 7 pm with a to-go drink bottle, and we'd take the train to our date spot for that night.

Besides the restaurants, my real favorite part about moving to NYC was getting to know my ex-wife's amazing family, and also her friends. Regarding the former, her aunt and uncle on her dad's side (her dad's brother) lived only a few blocks away from us with their two wonderful kids. Uncle D as we used to call him was like a mentor to me while I lived in NYC. We would frequently go running in Central Park and talk about business, sports, life, etc. A lawyer as well, Uncle D worked for a residential real estate company that owned numerous buildings throughout Manhattan. His wife's (at the time) family owned the company, which gave him a lot of flexibility to spend time with family, play golf, etc. Besides being one of the most genuinely kind people I have ever met, Uncle D's greatest trait is that, like my late father, he loved the finer things in life, such as a good meal, good wine, and good company. Countless times he would treat me and my ex (his niece) to dinner at some of Manhattan's best restaurants. I will never forget his gratitude, and I miss his companionship/mentorship. And his daughter at the time, fifteen going on thirty, quickly became one of my and my ex's best friends in NYC. Whenever my ex and I wanted a low-key night (e.g., dinner and a movie), we would invite her cousin to join us, and she often did.

After Uncle D, my ex-wife's other uncle on her father's side also lived right near us. An amazing person in his own right, he couldn't be more different than his brother Uncle D. Whereas Uncle D likes the finer things in life (expensive food, wine, clothes, jewelry, etc.), her other uncle on her dad's side (we'll call him Uncle M), is a lot like me and my ex in that although he also enjoys all that life has to offer, he is often able to find it for far less, which also often means a far more authentic/local experience. My fond memories with Uncle M include long bicycle rides through Manhattan (and New Jersey), Smorgasburg (a local foodie festival in Brooklyn), and BBQs at our apartment in the Upper East Side (or UES).

Last, but certainly not least, my ex's uncle on her mom's side (her mom's brother), Uncle I we'll call him, rounded out my new family in NYC. My ex often liked to say that I'm a combination of all three of her uncles, and Uncle I represented my "party" side. I remember the first time I met Uncle I, we met up for happy hour after work one Friday. While I was expecting a couple of low-key drinks and an early night, imagine my surprise when we ended up staying out all night and Uncle I woke up on our couch the next day. Besides being the party uncle, Uncle I, like my ex's two other two uncles, welcomed me into his family and home (literally) more than I could have ever hoped for. My fond memories with Uncle I include a Knicks/Bulls game at the Garden, more late nights, and several great nights at their beautiful house in Long Island. I miss Uncle I and his beautiful/kind wife as much as anyone in NYC. And finally, my ex's grandparents who also lived in Long Island at the time, also welcomed me into their home and had us over for several delicious meals, many of which were for the Jewish holidays.

Besides my ex's amazing family, perhaps my fondest memory of living in NYC was getting to live with a female partner for the first time, which allowed our relationship to blossom and ultimately led me to ask her to marry me (in Barcelona, Spain, where she studied abroad and claimed to be her favorite city in the world). For that reason alone, I will always have very fond memories of NYC, and under the right (and by right I mean inheriting $10 million) circumstances, I would not be opposed to moving back there one day. But as you know, this story takes another turn.

True to my word when I asked my ex to move to NYC with me, after about a year of living there and working for my NYC office, I began to get antsy again with my job. The initial excitement of moving to NYC, while still there, was beginning to wane. And consequently, the day-to-day grind of my mundane job was beginning to take a toll again. As such, my ex and I began to rekindle our discussions of traveling the world.

As I alluded to earlier, after about a year of living in NYC, my former roommate and one of my best friends took a RTW of his own. While on a road trip in Texas one weekend (my ex had a job in Austin so I met her there on a Thursday night and we rented a car and drove to San Antonio and Dallas for a long weekend, neither of which we had ever been to), I caught up with my old roommate and told him of our impending plans to follow in his footsteps. While our initial plan had been to simply quit our jobs and travel the world for about six months, in speaking to him, he informed me of a couple he met while traveling who found teaching jobs in Thailand, which they were thoroughly enjoying. Considering we were planning to spend most of our time traveling in Asia, particularly SE Asia, finding teaching jobs there suddenly sounded like a brilliant new idea. Instead of blowing through approximately $30-50K in six months and then returning to the States with nothing to show for it other than memories and pictures, working overseas would allow us to keep much more of our hard-saved money, while also allowing us the opportunity to stay overseas as long as we wanted. And perhaps best of all, we wouldn't have any gaps on our resumes, but rather, would gain additional work experience.

After learning that all it took for his friends to acquire these teaching jobs overseas was taking an online TEFL course, we were pretty much already sold. But then, by some sort of divine inspiration, we received a message confirming that this was our path. Typically, a TEFL course costs around $600 per person. But the VERY next day after talking to my old roommate and learning about this course, believe it or not, the daily Groupon (an online coupon/discount business that emails you a different daily deal every day) was for the TEFL course. And instead of $600, it was $70. Clearly, Big Brother (aka Verizon/Apple/Google) must have been listening to our conversation with my old roommate. Considering we both needed to take the course, this seemed like a no brainer, so we immediately purchased the Groupon (saving us over $1,000) and went to work. And by "we...went to work," I mean my ex-wife.

The TEFL course typically requires 120 hours online to complete it. For anyone that knows my ex, however, that equates to about 60 hours (she typically completes a given task in half the amount of time it should take). Considering I worked in an office all day and was responsible for billing around 50 hours per week (meaning you often had to be in the office closer to 70-80), she offered to take the course for me, and I wasn't about to complain. In truth, since she would already be taking the course for herself, it wasn't that much more difficult to open up a second computer (my computer), side by side with hers, and answer each question twice. It probably took her an extra 10-15 hours to take it for me as well. This was one of the many times in the next few months that I knew I would marry her (or at least ask her to marry me).[12]

Besides the possibility of generating new clients as a result of Hurricane Sandy, I also contemplated several other career changes before fully committing to the teaching abroad plan. For several years before resigning from my job, I looked for in-house counsel positions and other unique legal opportunities. But once we moved to NYC, the prospect of finding a new job became much more difficult because my cost of living went up dramatically (from approximately 60K/year in Chicago to 80-90K in NYC). As such, my options were much more limited. And one thing I always told myself was that I would never allow myself to just "break

---

[12] As an aside, I recall the day she completed the course for both of us. I came home from work and she was very excited to tell me something. As it so happened, I myself had been brainstorming something all day and was very excited to share the news with her. She suggested I go first, so I told her that in light of the recent Hurricane Sandy in New York, given my law practice (insurance recovery) and location in NYC, it provided me with a unique opportunity to possibly garner business for the first time in my professional career. If I could successfully do so, perhaps I would have a better chance at making partner, which would make the big law firm career much harder to walk away from (as an associate, I was making approximately $250,000 a year, which while certainly a great deal of money, pales in comparison to the approximately $500,000/year to over $1 million/year that income and equity partners make, respectively). Of course, as soon as I told her my thoughts, she broke down and cried of disappointment, rightfully so after all the hard work she put in to take the TEFL course for us. Her big news of the day had been to tell me she completed it. But after discussing further, she agreed that if I could use Hurricane Sandy as a launching pad to get new business, it might be worth sticking around NYC for a little while longer. And being the great partner that she was, not only did she morally support me with this decision, but she even helped me do research to find potential new clients. Of course, in the end, it was all for naught, as it turns out generating new (often Fortune 500 caliber or equivalent) clients, especially in NYC, is much harder than it sounds. And so it was back to Plan A: traveling and moving/working abroad.

even" being a lawyer. If I was going to break even, it was going to be doing something I greatly enjoyed, and for far fewer hours per week than the 50-60 I worked as a lawyer.

In the several years I was looking (though never seriously as I was far too busy working) for a new job, I recall only being mildly tempted by two other positions. The first was as an in-house lawyer position at a big insurance company in NYC, the second was as an in-house lawyer position with a medium sized insurance company in a small town in Pennsylvania. The former position paid only approximately $100,000/year, which in NYC, simply wouldn't cut it (at least not any more than just breaking even), so that was out. And the other position, although higher paying, was two hours from the nearest major airport, so that was out too. And so in the end, that's how I came to the conclusion to quit my high-paying, high-stressful, NYC job to travel the world and live abroad. Like I said, if I was going to break even, it was going to be doing something I liked doing (and I knew I liked teaching from my time in law school where I was a public speaking lecturer to undergraduate students) for the minimum number of hours possible.

So there we had it. The plan was in place. It was October 2012 and my ex and I had decided that we wanted to leave the country by the summer of 2013. Our plan was to travel over the summer and then find jobs starting in the Fall of 2013, ideally somewhere in Asia. We started by focusing on four countries, Thailand, China, Japan and South Korea. But after a little research and a number of inquiries (all done by my ex of course), we learned that being a teacher in China, Japan or South Korea meant working 40-50 hours/week, 50 weeks/year, basically the same lifestyle we were looking to leave. It's no wonder those countries are competing with the U.S. for global domination. Like the U.S., they work too hard.

Teachers in Thailand, on the other hand, only worked 15-20 hours/week and received 3-4 months paid vacation a year.

That was much more of what we were looking for. Moreover, Thailand is warm all year round, whereas northern Asia can be very cold in the winter. In addition to leaving the high hours/high stress lifestyle, we were also looking to leave the cold for a while, so Thailand seemed much more up our alley. Consequently, my ex's next task involved finding and reaching out to every single university or law school in Bangkok. Being the big city kid that I am and coming from NYC, we knew we wanted to live in Bangkok rather than some small town/city in Thailand. Additionally, I strongly preferred to teach university or graduate students rather than elementary or high school students, for it would look much better on my resume (especially if I wanted to try to become a law professor back in the States upon completing our travels, something I had been toying with), and also because I don't think I'd have the patience to teach children, especially young ones.

In the end, there are only approximately twenty universities and graduate schools in Bangkok, and my ex-wife reached out to all of them, as well as a couple of placement agencies that specialize in finding teaching jobs for foreigners wanting to live abroad, most of them for a small commission. While we only heard back from a few schools, that was more than enough for our needs. Our only requirement other than being in or very close to Bangkok, was of course that they hire both of us, which we didn't expect to be a problem considering we heard that foreign schools typically prefer to hire couples, as they tend to last longer than single people. After a few different Skype calls (Zoom also wasn't a thing back then), we felt pretty good about our chances with a couple of different schools and agencies, but we really had our hopes pinned on one particular school in Bangkok.

After perusing their website and Skyping with the hiring coordinators, this school sounded perfect. It had two different campuses, one in the city of Bangkok and one about an hour outside of the city. We would be teaching at the suburban campus (where almost all English classes are taught), but in addition to a monthly salary that was more than enough to live on ($1,200 for me because I had a graduate degree, and $800 for my ex, with essentially no tax), we would also *each* receive free housing. Yes, two different free accommodations. Since each teacher receives free accommodation, and since we were two teachers, we would each receive our own accommodation, which was essentially a dorm room on the suburban campus. Yep, we were headed back to college!

While initially hesitant about the prospect of living an hour outside of Bangkok, we figured with free housing, we could get a hotel in the city every weekend and still be able to save money. And that's exactly what we did for our first couple of months teaching, that is, until we realized that instead of getting two free dorm rooms at their suburban campus (one of which we made our bedroom and the other of which we made the living room/kitchen), we could take one free room at the suburban campus, where we would stay during the week, and another free room at the school's city campus, the latter in a local residential apartment complex, rather than a dorm room. So after two months of living in the burbs and staying in hotels on the weekends, we decided to take one free room in the burbs and one free apartment in the city. That's right, within two months of living in Bangkok, we had two free apartments. And best of all, our school provided free transportation between the two campuses (about a forty-five-minute drive).

But first, I'm getting ahead of myself. Before settling on our school, a brief story cemented our desire to work there, much like the daily Groupon deal cemented our path to become English teachers abroad. While at a wedding in Arizona for one of my good friends from college, we sat at a table with one of his good friends from high school, a guy by the name of "Runaway Jim." I knew Runaway Jim from being friends/roommates with my friend who was getting married, and while I generally liked him, I will always remember when I woke up in college in the middle of the night one night to find him pissing...in my closet. Anyways, Runaway's date at the wedding was a girl I had never met before. But after briefly talking with her, my ex and I learned that she recently came back from teaching English in Thailand. And where else other than the school we had set our sights on! Needless to say, we spent the rest of the night pestering her with questions, to which her answers further fueled our desire to work there.

Once we received our offers to work at our dream school in early 2013, we seriously set in motion the myriad of other things we needed to take care of before leaving the US indefinitely. Among other things, we needed to rent (again) or sell my condo, sell both my furniture in Chicago and our furniture in NYC, plan our summer trip around the world and book our flights/tours before arriving in Thailand, quit our jobs (mine at my law firm and my ex's with her brother, both of which required extreme delicacy and timing), and oh yeah, lastly...get married.

I'll save the whole getting married part of our story for the section below wherein I discuss Practical Impairments to Finding Happiness, but suffice to say, just as we planned our entire RTW 1.0 and all of the steps leading up to it (e.g., taking our TEFL course, finding teaching jobs, etc.), my ex's mom took the laboring oar (both time-wise and financially) in planning our wedding. And oh what a beautiful wedding it was, at her parents' home and in their own backyard. Some people who attended it said it was the most beautiful wedding they had ever been to. But while my ex's mom was busy planning our wedding (seeking our approval on all big issues of course—e.g., rabbi, food, etc.), we were busy planning our RTW 1.0.

First and foremost, for our RTW 1.0., we knew we wanted to do a Mt. Everest Base Camp ("EBC") trek, and so we pretty much planned our entire RTW 1.0 around that. The best time to hike Everest is from September to December, but since we needed to start teaching in Thailand in September (or so we thought--more on that below), we were planning to hike Everest in late August, a small risk, but one we had to take. I often used to joke (partially true however) that the real reason I quit my job is because I've always wanted to hike EBC and it takes two weeks, presumably without internet the entire time. And while I could likely get two weeks off work (though that would constitute my entire vacation for the year), going two weeks without being able to check my work email would be nearly impossible (or at best, an absolute nightmare upon returning to work after the trek). And so the first thing we booked for our RTW 1.0 was an EBC trek, and boy was I excited.[13]

After Everest, we quickly started to put together the rest of our trip, which started with a month in South America as follows: 1) a week in Peru visiting Machu Picchu via a 3 night/4 day hike of the Inca Trail and a 3 night/4 day stay in the Peruvian Amazon; 2) two days in Iguazu Falls with a day on the Brazilian side and a day on the Argentinean side; 3) three days in Florianopolis, Brazil's beach capital; 4) two days in Punta del Este and two days in Montevideo, Uruguay; 5) three days in Mendoza, Argentina (where they make Malbec, the famous wine); and lastly 6) five days in Buenos Aires.

---

[13] In hindsight, if we could do it again, we likely would not have booked a trek in advance with a tour company, as once we arrived, we realized we likely could have done the trek for about half the price ($600 versus $1,200 per person) had we waited to book everything until we arrived. But this only works in the low/off season, and being the OCD planners that we were (not to mention, as I said, I basically quit my job for this trek), we simply had to book ahead. But for anyone else thinking of doing an EBC trek, heed this advice.

After South America, we would spend a week in India doing the Golden Triangle (a few days in Delhi, a couple of days in Agra visiting the Taj Mahal, and a few days in Jaipur). Following India, we would head to Nepal where we would undertake an eleven-day EBC trek, followed by a few days of sightseeing in Kathmandu, Nepal. Finally, we would head to SE Asia, starting with a few days in Bangkok getting situated with our new jobs, before heading out again to visit Cambodia for ten days (Sihanoukville, Siem Reap and the famous Angkor Wat, and the capital Phnom Penh) and Laos for a week (the capital Vientiane, Vang Vieng and Luang Prabang).

All in all, the three-month itinerary would take us to nine different countries on two different continents, ten countries and three continents if you consider Seattle, WA and Portland, OR in the Pacific Northwest of the United States where we started our journey. When it was all said and done, our RTW 1.0[14] went swimmingly well, minus a couple of minor hiccups, one unpreventable and the other unfortunate. The unpreventable hiccup involved our bus from Mendoza to Santiago, Chile being cancelled because of poor weather (it was winter in South America), which resulted in our being unable to visit Chile. As sad as we were to miss seeing Chile, the primary reason we wanted to go there was to ski in the Andes, so we weren't too dismayed because we were able to re-route our itinerary to ski at Las Lenas, the largest ski resort in Argentina.

---

[14] I say RTW 1.0 because unlike our original plan of traveling the world for six months to a year, under our new plan, we would start our life-changing journey with the aforementioned three-month trip (RTW 1.0), then the following summer we would travel through the rest of SE Asia (Vietnam, Philippines, Indonesia, Singapore, Malaysia and Brunei), all while being paid by our school (aka RTW 2.0). And finally, the summer after that (2015) we would travel to Northern Asia (China, Japan, Korea, and Taiwan), again using our funds from teaching (aka RTW 3.0).

The unfortunate hiccup also happened in Argentina when upon arriving in Buenos Aires, my ex-wife handed her bag to a man who pretended to work for the hostel we were staying at (why she thought our hostel would have a bellhop, I know not). Of course, he didn't work there but rather took off with her bag down the street. Fortunately, the bag consisted solely of her clothes, nothing of real value (e.g., no electronics, jewelry, etc.) and remarkably not even the heavy winter clothes she needed for our upcoming Everest trek. Also fortunately, we were able to file a successful insurance claim which not only recouped almost our entire insurance premium, but also allowed her to purchase an entire new wardrobe in Bangkok (with plenty of money left over afterwards).[15] In short, our RTW 1.0 (aka the Bucket List trip) was the trip of a lifetime, or as I like to refer to it, the trip of ten thousand lifetimes, because not everyone gets to take this type of trip over the course of their life. Rather, probably only 1 in 10,000 people (and that's only of the people who can afford it, and largely non-Americans), or likely far less.

Among the many highlights from our RTW 1.0, besides the obvious hike to EBC, trekking the Inca Trail and seeing Machu Picchu was probably one of the coolest things I've ever done (and the latter was probably the single most

---

[15] As a comic aside, after we filed a police report, I took my ex-wife on a "shopping spree" for new clothes in Buenos Aires. After 2-3 stores and still having not purchased anything (my ex was more frugal than me), she said something to the effect of "these [jeans] don't fit perfectly." Subsequently, I immediately told the store clerk "well take two of them" and proceeded to tell my ex she had two hours to replenish her wardrobe before I moved on to the rest of our Buenos Aires itinerary, but rest assured, we weren't spending the next 3-4 days (or even hours) shopping for clothes in what, notwithstanding the unfortunate aforementioned incident, actually became our favorite city in South America, by far.

71

impressive thing I've ever seen),[16] Iguazu Falls was almost just as mesmerizing and awe-inspiring,[17] cruising down the Amazon watching pink dolphins and fishing for piranha was certainly unforgettable (though I could have lived without the relentless mosquitoes), gorging on steak sandwiches and parrilla (the latter is an Argentinean specialty consisting of various meats, typically steak, chicken, liver, kidneys, intestines and blood sausage)[18] in Montevideo (Uruguay) and Buenos Aires and bicycling through the wineries of Mendoza[19] were certainly the highlights of South America.

---

[16] Thankfully my ex-wife was able to see it as well for she woke up the morning of our trek not feeling well and at one point, less than ten minutes before departure, said she wasn't going to make it. Fortunately, I was able to convince her to give it a go, and though it was tough sledding at the beginning, she prevailed like the trooper that she always was.

[17] And we also got to become good friends with a Romanian flight attendant from Dubai whom for a while had us convinced he was an Arabian Prince.

[18] Parrilla is so good that my ex-wife and I thought briefly about opening a parrilla restaurant in the U.S., which for the life of us, we couldn't figure out why it didn't already exist or if it did, we hadn't seen it (and for the record, it's very different than the Brazilian/Argentinean steakhouses that offer all you can eat meat on skewers).

[19] As it so happened, the one day we wanted to do the bicycle tour was Election Day in Argentina, which meant the tour was closed for the day. This happens once every four years in Argentina. Needless to say, it was a tense couple of hours as we had to rearrange our plans and rush out to the wineries to make sure we partook in this must-do activity. This was not the last time our timing for a trip would coincide with something that happens only once a year, or less. On our RTW 2.0, we just happened to be in Manila, the capital of the Philippines, for their national Independence Day, and we inadvertently traveled through Indonesia and Malaysia, predominantly Muslim countries, during all of Ramadan. The latter was only mildly problematic until Hari Raya, the last few days of Ramadan, when literally everything shut down and we had to buy a last minute flight to avoid getting stuck in a desolate town. But Hari Raya made up for it in Brunei where we were able to visit (and feast at for free) the Sultan's palace (literally), which is only open to the general public three days a year during that time.

In India, seeing the Taj Mahal was certainly a sight to behold, though the Delhi Belly had already gotten to me by that point, which resulted in my literally throwing up inside the Taj Mahal.[20] Angkor Wat in Siem Reap was as, if not more, impressive than the Taj. And drinking our first whiskey/red bull bucket ($1.50), eating our first seafood BBQ ($3) and smoking our first shisha on the beaches of Sihanoukville (Cambodia), were a welcome delight, as was our $5/night adjacent beachside guesthouse. Finally, tubing down the river in Vang Vieng (a notorious party town where expat revelers stop at various bars along the river and relive their glorious college/drinking years) and exploring the French colonial streets of Luang Prabang were our highlights in Lao. All in all, it was everything we had hoped for and more. I think my ex-wife put it best when at one point on our trip (at Iguazu Falls, which we saw from both the Argentinian and Peruvian side) she said, "Every day of this trip I'm seeing the most beautiful thing I've ever seen."

My response: "Mission accomplished."

After completing our RTW 2.0, which is when I began writing this book, I can honestly say those were some of the happiest times of my life. I was in my favorite part of the world (Southeast Asia), spending every day with, at the time, the love of my life, and seeing and doing new things every day that most people can only dream about. And best of all, for the first time in my life, I didn't dread the thought of going to work every day (nor did I dread the thought of returning to work after three months of vacation). In fact, I actually looked forward to it.

---

[20] I'm still not sure if it was a result of a) the combination of chicken tikka masala and rogen josh the waiter warned me not to get; b) spoiled yogurt left out a breakfast buffet; or c) non-alcoholic beer we inadvertently bought at a local pop-up shop, or perhaps a combination of all three. Regardless fortunately I only threw up in the grounds/gardens of the Taj Mahal and not the actual temple itself.

In addition to enjoying teaching, I was living in my favorite country in the world (Thailand), and because it was still foreign, it seemed like I was on vacation every day (even though we had lived there for over a year and had two separate homes there). And as my ex-wife always liked to say, every semester we had new classes, new students and got a new schedule, so unlike my previous job which was excruciatingly monotonous, mundane and boring, teaching in Bangkok never got boring because we were always doing something new, with new people at new times and still in a relatively new-feeling country. And of course, when you only work 15-20 hours/week and get four months of paid vacation per year, no job can be that bad. And that my friends, is what I like to call professional happiness. It's the first time in my life I'd ever felt it, and man did it feel good.

For those who are interested, highlights of our RTW 2.0 included 1) drinking the cheapest beer in the world (with a blind guy who shared a local "bong") and eating dog (called thit cho) in Hanoi and Ho Chi Minh, Vietnam; 2) spending the night on a luxury boat in Halong Bay (for my birthday no less); 3) swimming in the pitch black for forty-five minutes through a cave in the Phong Nha National Park (also Vietnam), home to the largest cave in the world; 4) hiking through the rice terraces of the northern Philippines and sleeping in local villages along the way (killing a local chicken for dinner); 5) snorkeling with giant whale sharks and giant sea turtles in Cebu and Negros (Philippines), respectively; 6) surfing in Bali (though next time maybe we won't break the board); 7) hiking Gunung Rinjani, one of the tallest (and certainly the most breathtaking) volcanoes in Lombok, Indonesia for three days; 8) relaxing in the Gili Islands after that; 9) waking up at 3 am to catch the sunrise view of Gunung Bromo (on the back of a local's motorcycle which included a sketchy "border" crossing); 10) spending a week with my ex's mom in the first-class cities of Singapore and Kuala Lumpor; 11) summiting Mt. Kinabalu in

Malaysian Borneo, the highest mountain in maritime Southeast Asia outside of Papua; 12) scuba diving in Sipadan (also Malaysian Borneo), frequently voted one of the top five diving sites in the world, and justifiably so as we saw literally hundreds of sharks and giant sea turtles in our two days of diving there;[21] and 13) visiting the aforementioned Sultan's palace in Brunei, which is only open three days a year to the general public, which just happened to coincide with the three days we were there.

The above narrative was just a small taste of the many sights and wonders that my ex-wife and I experienced over our first 1.5 years abroad. If you're interested in a more detailed description, as well as our itinerary and adventures from our RTW 3.0 which included 2 weeks in Japan, two weeks in Taiwan and five weeks in China, or our many travels throughout Thailand during our four years of living there, feel free to visit our travel blog at **thestavediaries.com**.

---

[21] To dive Sipadan, you typically need to book months in advance (which we did) because they only have a limited number (120) of permits per day. And when you book, you typically need to book 2-3 days' worth of diving, with only one day being at Sipadan and the other(s) being at nearby, local islands, of their choosing. To our skeptical delight, however, when we arrived, we were granted an extra day at Sipadan because there had been a lot of last-minute cancellations in light of a recent shooting/kidnapping by Filipino "pirates" at a nearby island. Thankfully, we didn't see any pirates while we were there. Just tons of sharks, turtles and other amazing marine life.

Part Four
The Convincing Your Family and Friends Stage

I think we like to complicate things when it is really quite simple: find what it is that makes you happy and who it is that makes you happy and you're set. I promise.

Even after you've overcome the enormous hurdle of convincing yourself of the merit of doing away with the traditional American notions of happiness (e.g., corporate job, big family, house in the suburbs, nice car, etc.) in lieu of finding the aforementioned personal and professional happiness, for those of you that are lucky enough to have people who care about you, you still have another major obstacle to overcome: convincing your family and friends. For me, that was easy. For years, my parents had heard me gripe about how I hated my job and how I yearned for something more in life. As you may recall, when I originally started working in big firm law right out of law school, my mom predicted I would last three years, the typical jumping ship point for most big firm attorneys. In reality, I lasted eight years, so I think I did okay.

My parents also saw me struggle with finding love, dating many women over the years but none "forever" worthy. So I don't think they were all too surprised when my ex and I called them one day, shortly before my engagement proposal, to tell them of our impending journey. Of course, they asked lots of good, tough questions as any good parent should do, but in the end, they were completely supportive of our decision. Plus, they would finally have a reason to visit Thailand, a place they had always wanted to visit.

My ex-wife's parents, on the other hand, I knew would take a little more convincing. Maybe it's because they're from Ohio (a traditionally more conservative state), or maybe it's because my parents are very liberal, but I knew convincing my ex's parents of the merit of our idea would not be easy. Fortunately, we were not asking for their permission, but rather, just seeking their support and approval. I'll never forget when we flew home to Columbus shortly after getting engaged to tell them of our plans. It was the dead of winter in Columbus, OH, the middle of America (i.e., it was freezing). In their minds, we were probably flying home to tell them of our grand plans for their daughter's wedding.

Like a typical Jewish girl, that would entail a year or more engagement, a huge flashy wedding with hundreds of people costing upwards of $100,000, and likely a short honeymoon to an exotic island followed by a return to our normal, mundane, corporate America jobs and lives (the type I described earlier in this book; two kids and a house in the suburbs after a brief stint in the "big city"). I can only imagine their shock and awe when instead, we told them that we were quitting our jobs (and for my ex, since she worked with her brother, that would mean a huge blow for him and hence her parents' son), traveling the world for three months, and moving to Thailand for a year or more. Oh, and as for that whole wedding thing, we were postponing that until our return.

My ex's dad was his stoic, yet thought-provoking, usual self. Her mom, not surprisingly, was much more animated. After jointly telling them of our plans, I decided to give them some time alone, which meant I retreated to the bleak, winter wonderland of Ohio. After thirty minutes of walking in circles outside, I reluctantly returned, delighted to find out I was still a welcomed member of the family (or soon to be member). In the end, my ex's parents were also fully supportive of our decision, with one big caveat: they strongly preferred we get married before we leave the country.

Though we hadn't really ever considered that (mainly because there were a million things we needed to do to prepare for our journey, and getting married was not on that list), after further contemplation, we agreed that it was in everyone's best interests (ourselves included) to get married before we left the US. For safety reasons (e.g., making medical decisions on each other's behalves), practical reasons (e.g., border crossings, passport control, etc.) and the simple fact that we loved each other and, at the time, wanted to spend the rest of our lives together, we all agreed that getting married before we left the U.S. was a good (and arguably necessary) idea.

After that, the rest of the pre-travel plans started falling into place, one step at a time. For 6-8 months before we left, every night, I would come home from work and my ex would tell me what she had researched that day. From flights, to tours, to visas, to necessary vaccinations, to job searching in Asia, to the additional state bars I was applying to before our departure, to her daily TEFL progress, to selling our furniture, to the countless decisions we had to make regarding our wedding (though as previously mentioned, thankfully, her mom took the laboring oar in terms of the wedding, and it turned out blissfully), the list was literally endless. And fortunately, because my ex worked for herself and also from home, she was able to do a little bit each and every day, and then every night when I got home from work, she would report on her progress and we would discuss any outstanding issues. We did this for 6-8 months. And every time we crossed something off the list, something else would get added. In a way, this was a great test for our impending marriage, for it required an enormous amount of teamwork, cooperation, and to some extent (mostly by my ex), sacrifice and compromise, all essential ingredients to any successful marriage.

After our parents, slowly, we began telling our closest friends of our impending plans as well. It was a little tricky, however, as I wasn't planning to tell my law firm of my resignation until a few weeks before our departure. I went back and forth about how much notice I should give, but ultimately decided three weeks seemed like a fair amount. Mainly, I just wanted to be sure I received my yearly bonus (due in mid-April), and also allow myself enough time to wrap up all my ongoing projects and transition them to my colleagues. In short, I wanted to be sure to leave on good terms without shortchanging myself in any way.

As we began to tell our friends, most were in awe, many were jealous, and a few (or maybe more) thought we were flat out crazy. The ones who really knew us, however, I don't think were all too surprised, being the somewhat unconventional trailblazers that we are/were. For those that were still skeptical, I'd often refer them to a number of inspirational quotes that I compiled in the months leading up to our RTW 1.0. I collected them in part for the purpose of convincing others of the merit of our adventure, but also for my own self-validation. All of them, in some form or another, validate the choice we made and hopefully will inspire others to make a similar leap, particularly for anyone already on the edge and just in need of that extra push. In no particular order, they are as follows:[1]

- When you're young, you have all the time in the world and no money. When you're old, you have all of the money in the world and no time.

- Imagine life is a game in which you are juggling five balls. The balls are called work, family, health, friends and integrity. And you're keeping all of them in the air. But one day you finally come to understand that work is a rubber ball. If you drop it, it will bounce back. The other four balls...are made of glass. If you drop one of these, it will be irrevocably scoffed, nicked, perhaps even shattered. – James Patterson

---

[1] Where known, I've listed the source.

- The greatest risk in life is not taking one.
- Life is for spontaneous laughter, grand adventures, eating ice cream and finding love.
- The craziest part of RTW travel is that so many people think it's out of reach for them. Yet people waste money constantly on things that don't make them happy. In life, you can buy things or you can buy experiences. I have found that experiences make me much happier. For the cost of a used car, you can actually go see the world. All it takes is the courage to dream big and then set goals and make it happen.
- Twenty years from now you will be more disappointed by the things you didn't do than the things you did. So throw off the bow lines. Sail away from the safe harbor. Catch the trade winds in your sails. Explore. Dream. Discover. – Mark Twain
- Please be a traveler, not a tourist. Try new things, meet new people, and look beyond what's right in front of you. Those are the keys to understanding this amazing world we live in. – Andrew Zimmern
- Take leaps of faith. Even when you don't know where you are going to land. You are going to develop so much courage and trust in yourself as you take risks. It's okay not to be 100% sure. 51% sure is enough to take the leap. – Christine Hassler
- Nobody on their deathbed has ever said "I just wish I went into the office one more day." Even Steve Jobs, though Elon Musk might ☺.
- The best day of your life is the one on which you decide life is your own. No apologies or excuses. No one to lean on, rely on or blame. The gift is yours. It is an amazing journey. And you alone are responsible for the quality of it. This is the day your life really begins. – Bob Moawad
- If you think adventure is dangerous, try routine. It is lethal. – Paulo Coelho

80

- I think we like to complicate things when it is really quite simple: find what it is that makes you happy and who it is that makes you happy and you're set. I promise.
- What you do every day matters more than what you do every once in a while. – Gretchen Rubin
- Travel is fatal to prejudice, bigotry, and narrow-mindedness, and many of our people need it sorely on these accounts. Broad, wholesome, charitable views of men and things cannot be acquired by vegetating in one little corner of the Earth all of one's lifetime. – Mark Twain.
- I am not what happened to me. I am what I choose to become! – Carl Jung
- The trick is to enjoy life. Don't wish away your days, waiting for better one's ahead. – Marjorie Pay Hinckley
- If we wait until we're ready, we'll be waiting for the rest of our lives. – Lemony Snicket
- The price of anything is the amount of life you exchange for it – Henry Thoreau
- Don't wait for your ship to come in. Swim out and meet it. – Gary Wood
- It's the scariest choices that end up being the most worthwhile. – Melissa Joy Kong
- I don't know where I'm going from here, but I promise it won't be boring. – David Bowie
- For whatever it's worth, it's never too late to be whoever you want to be. I hope you live a life you're proud of, and if you find that you're not, I hope you have the strength to start over. – F. Scott Fitzgerald
- Travel is never a matter of money, but of courage.
- We travel not to escape life, but for life not to escape us.

- Success is doing what you want to do, when you want, where you want, with whom you want, as much as you want.[2] – Tony Robins
- For the past 33 years, I have looked in the mirror every morning and asked myself: "If today were the last day of my life, would I want to do what I am about to do today?" And whenever the answer has been "No" for too many days in a row, I know I need to change something... – Steve Jobs
- Your life does not get better by chance. It gets better by change.
- If you don't like where you are, then move on. You're not a tree.
- Everything you want is on the other side of fear. – Jack Canfield
- My goal is to build a life I don't need a vacation from. – Rob Hill Sr.
- Become friends with people who aren't your age. Hang out with people whose first language is not the same as yours. Get to know someone who doesn't come from your social class. This is how you see the world. This is how you grow.
- Life is like a camera. Focus on what's important. Capture the good times. Develop from the negatives. And if things don't work out, take another shot.
- You can't make someone else's choices so you shouldn't let someone else make yours. Follow your heart.
- Happiness is a journey, not a destination.
- One day your life will flash before your eyes. Make sure it's worth watching.

---

[2] Recall earlier I said the word "success" has several meanings which would be used interchangeably herein. In my view, this is a far better definition of the word than the traditional meaning which implies monetary wealth.

- If work were so pleasant, the rich would keep it for themselves. – Mark Twain
- Remembering you are going to die is the best way I know to avoid the trap of thinking you have something to lose. You are already naked. There is no reason not to follow your heart. – Steve Jobs, Stanford commencement address 2005
- In a chronically leaking boat, energy devoted to changing vessels is more productive than energy devoted to patching leaks. – Warren Buffett
- Nobody can go back and start a new beginning, but anyone can start today and make a new ending. – Maria Robinson
- A year from now you will wish you had started today. – Karen Lamb
- It doesn't matter where you are, you are nowhere compared to where you can go. – Bob Proctor
- Never too old, never too bad, never too late, never too sick to start from scratch once again. – Bikram Choudhury.
- Don't say you don't have enough time. You have exactly the same number of hours per day that were given to Helen Keller, Pasteur, Michelangelo, Mother Teresa, Leonardo da Vinci, Thomas Jefferson, and Albert Einstein. – Life's Little Instruction Book
- By changing nothing, nothing changes. – Tony Robbins
- Sometimes good things fall apart so better things can fall together. – Marilyn Monroe
- If what you're doing is not your passion, you have nothing to lose.
- The best thing you can do is the right thing; the next best thing you can do is the wrong thing; the worst thing you can do is nothing. – Theodore Roosevelt
- If you do what you've always done, you'll get what you've always gotten. – Tony Robbins

- The greatest mistake you can make in life is to be continually fearing you will make one. – Elbert Hubbard
- If you run you stand a chance of losing, but if you don't run you've already lost. – Barack Obama
- You have to do what is right for yourself. Nobody else is walking in your shoes.
- If you focus on results, you'll never change. If you focus on change, you will get results. – Jack Dixon
- The best project you will ever work on is you.
- All our dreams can come true—If we have the courage to pursue them. – Walt Disney
- If opportunity doesn't knock, build a door. – Milton Berle
- I'd rather be a failure at something I love than a success at something I hate. –George Burns
- If you don't go after what you want, you'll never have it. If you don't ask, the answer is always no. If you don't step forward, you're always in the same place. – Nora Roberts
- You can never cross the ocean until you have the courage to lose sight of the shore. – Christopher Columbus
- Life should not be a journey to the grave with the intention of arriving safely in a pretty and well preserved body, but rather to skid in broadside in a cloud of smoke, thoroughly used up, totally worn out, and loudly proclaiming "Wow! What a Ride!"
- If I'm an advocate for anything, it's to move. As far as you can, as much as you can. Across the ocean, or simply across the river. The extent to which you can walk in someone else's shoes or at least eat their food, it's a plus for everybody – Anthony Bourdain
- Your body is not a temple, it's an amusement park. Enjoy the ride. – Anthony Bourdain
- If you're twenty-two, physically fit, hungry to learn and be better, I urge you to travel - as far and as

widely as possible. Sleep on floors if you have to. Find out how other people live and eat and cook. Learn from them - wherever you go. – Anthony Bourdain

- Drink heavily with locals whenever possible. – Anthony Bourdain
- Travel isn't always pretty. It isn't always comfortable. Sometimes it hurts, it even breaks your heart. But that's okay. The journey changes you; it should change you. It leaves marks on your memory, on your consciousness, on your heart, and on your body. You take something with you. Hopefully, you leave something good behind. – Anthony Bourdain
- A salary is the drug they give you to forget your dreams. - Kevin O'Leary
- The new flex isn't a lambo, big house and Rolex. It's freedom—time freedom, financial freedom and location freedom.
- It doesn't matter how much money you make. If you need permission to take a day off, then it's not enough.
- I actually don't want to climb any corporate ladders. I don't care about job titles. I don't need accolades. I just want to have enough income to fund my lifestyle, not be depressed, help other people and be around good human beings. That's it.
- Don't be fooled by the illusion of wealth. Big houses, fancy cars, designer clothes, extravagant holidays are not wealth. It's most likely debt. Wealth is freedom, options, time and health.
- When someone asks what my dream job is. Literally nothing. Who dreams to have a job. My only passion is to travel and eat good food.
- Get out of your hometown. It doesn't have to be forever. Move. Travel. Explore. See the world.

There's more than life than the same 10 people and 2 bars.

- An entire generation believed this is the American Dream—work 40-60 hours/week, $100K+ on a degree we hardly need, own a car we can barely afford, 2 weeks a year away from work, and retire in your 60s when you're old and tired. Is this really the dream life?
- "I don't want a nation of thinkers, I want a nation of workers." --John D. Rockefeller. That's why Americans aren't taught financial literary in school.
- "Think of yourself as dead. You have already lived your life. Now take what's left of it and live it properly." –Marcus Aurelius (aka Russell Crowe's character in Gladiator)
- If you have the means and opportunity, don't stay in one tiny little corner of the entire world and call that a life.
- In the end, it's not the years in your life that count. It's the life in your years. –Abraham Lincoln
- The highest form of wealth is the ability to wake up every day and say "I can do whatever I want today."
- The last one is not so much a quote but rather a story that my mom sent me one day. It came from a Dear Amy column in the Chicago Tribune. A woman wrote Amy and told her that she and her husband were contemplating quitting their jobs, selling all of their possessions and traveling the world. Her friends and family, however, not surprisingly, thought she was crazy. She wanted advice from Amy. Amy replied by sharing a story from another couple who had taken a similar trip in the past. The couple said that throughout their travels, they encountered several older couples taking a similar trip, and in talking to them, one consistent scenario seemed to keep recurring: the older woman would say that she originally planned to take

86

the trip with her first husband, but then he died, so she ended up taking the trip with her second husband. Needless to say, Abby supported her decision. And also needless to say, I didn't want to be that first husband.

Part Five
The Acceptance, Letting Go and Saying Goodbye Stage

In response to my resignation, everyone at my law firm was overwhelmingly supportive. Of the many positive responses I received, one that stuck out the most was "I wish I had the courage when I was your age to do what you're doing."

After all the planning (6-8 months total), the nervousness of telling our parents, our friends, and most importantly, our employers, we were finally ready to embark on our adventure. Oh, but first, we had to do one small thing: get married.

The wedding was a smashing success (thank you to my ex mother-in-law). The mini-moon to Washington DC and Baltimore was super fun (in order to keep our plan a secret until it was time to give my notice, I had to tell everyone that we were going on a mini-moon right after our wedding, but that we'd be taking a longer honeymoon later in the Fall or winter). For anyone that knows me, a honeymoon to DC and Baltimore just wouldn't cut it.

After finally giving my resignation to my law firm three weeks before our departure, it felt like a giant weight had been lifted off my shoulders. For six months, it felt like I was leading a double life. Although I continued to dutifully fulfill all of my obligations to both my clients and my law firm, my mind was completely consumed by our impending RTW (how could it not be). Not only was telling my law firm of my impending plan a huge relief, but so was their collective response. Almost unanimously, from the main partner I worked most closely with and to whom I gave my initial notice, to my practice group leader in another city, to other partners I worked with, to other associates, and even down to the paralegals, secretaries and other support staff, everyone was universally in awe of and inspired by my life-changing decision. Perhaps behind closed doors they were saying "he's crazy" or "boy he'll probably regret that down the road," but to my face, they were saying things like "I'm jealous," "I wish I had the courage when I was your age to do what you're doing," and one partner even said "When I was your age, my wife and I talked about doing something similar, but ultimately we chickened out." Even my opposing counsel in one case (a very senior partner) said "That's the best resignation story I've ever heard."

But perhaps the most encouraging response I received came from a secretary I never met who responded to my mass email on my last day of work saying goodbye and thank you. In her email, she told me that her lifelong dream had always been to visit Mt. Everest, but that unfortunately, it was a dream she'd likely never realize (she neglected to tell me why, but it was likely due to the same family and financial commitments that bog most people down, as discussed further below). She said she'd live vicariously through me, and even look for me at Base Camp through a Google Maps program. All this from a woman I'd never even met. Suddenly, my life-changing decision was looking better and better.

In the three weeks between giving my resignation and leaving the States indefinitely, I made plans to visit with all of my closest friends and family. Although my ex and I never put a timetable on our return to the States, I think in everyone's mind, they were under the impression we'd only be gone a year or so. My ex and I, however, had other thoughts. Almost everyone we had talked to who took a trip similar to ours (particularly to SE Asia) had the same story: they either moved there with the intention of only staying a year but ended up staying much longer, or they hadn't intended on moving there at all, but rather, were just traveling through, and ended up moving there indefinitely.

While my ex and I hadn't put too much thought into it (we were really trying to just go with the flow and embrace the whole experience), I think both of us were operating under the assumption that we'd be gone for at least a few years if not more, whether entirely in Thailand/SE Asia, or elsewhere. Thus, it was a bittersweet feeling saying goodbye to my friends and family. My family I knew I would video chat with at least once a week and they would also be visiting. My friends, on the other hand, I knew I might not see for a very long time (not to mention several, and eventually eight in total, of my friends would be getting married the first year I was gone). Such is life I guess. As Red (aka Morgan Freeman) in *Shawshank Redemption* so aptly said, "get busy living, or get busy dying."

Although I tried my best to prepare myself for and also get excited about our RTW 1.0 and move to Thailand, it really didn't hit me until we were on our first plane ride to Portland, Oregon, or maybe even a few days later when we flew from Seattle to Lima, Peru. Try as I did, I think I was simply too busy making all of the necessary last-minute arrangements, or maybe I just couldn't come to grips with the fact that I actually had the guts and wherewithal (the latter mostly my ex) to pull it off, to get psyched up for the trip before we left. And guts notwithstanding, I was still a ball of nerves leading up to the trip, constantly questioning whether I was making the right decision (namely quitting a $250,000/year job in a shitty job market to take a job for $10,000/year with a very uncertain future) and also constantly wondering whether we'd be safe throughout our trip and also whether we'd enjoy living/working in Thailand. But once we were on that first plane, all of those fears and doubts quickly vanquished, for we were about to embark on the trip of "ten thousand lifetimes."

Part Six
Practical Impairments to Finding Happiness

For a middle-class American family, it is estimated to cost approximately $241,000 to raise a child from birth to the age of eighteen. And that doesn't include the cost of college, nor the cost of any private education or even daycare/babysitting, before the age of eighteen.

Now that I've walked you through all of the conceptual and theoretical impairments to taking your own RTW, or just taking your own alternative path towards happiness, there are several practical impairments that typically prevent Americans from taking a leap such as mine. In my many years of traveling, I've talked to countless other travelers from all over the world, and rest assured, the practical impairment discussed below are *strictly American impairments*. No other country in the world subjects itself to such impairments, at least on the scale of and to the degree that Americans do. And when I talk about these impairments to people from other countries, they are in shock that Americans do these things on such a regular basis and to such an extraordinary degree.[1]

---

[1] As suggested earlier, my story is just one story, but I encourage and urge you to create your own. Whether your passion is travel (like mine), starting a business, reading, working out, writing a book (which I only had time for once I left the corporate America rat race), pursuing a new hobby or trade, taking a cooking class, starting a blog, etc., many Americans are never able to pursue their passions simply because they don't have the time due to the rigors of their everyday life. As explained

As you read this, many of you may think that these "impairments" are actually necessities. And though to some degree some of them may be, most of them are in fact luxuries. And even to the extent they're considered necessities for you, there is no need to spend the ridiculous amount of money that many Americans often spend on these things. Rather, many of these things can be had for far less. But as a good friend of mine recently pointed out to me, for many Americans, particularly those caught in the corporate American rat race that consumes so many Americans, they indulge in these things primarily to mask their unhappiness with their everyday lives. Whether it's something as significant as a car or as simple as a piece of clothing or jewelry, many Americans buy these things solely to make themselves feel better about their everyday lives. And the irony is, it's precisely because of their everyday lives that they're often unable to even enjoy these purchases, or at least enjoy them to the extent it merits their purchase. And ironically their continued purchase all but guarantees they'll continue to live a life of primarily work rather than personal satisfaction.

Student Debt

Although briefly discussed earlier, the first major impairment to leading an alternative lifestyle from that of the typical 9-5, 50 week/year American "rat race" lifestyle, is student debt. The cost of college in the United States compared to other

---

above, these rigors are strictly American rigors, as almost all other first-world countries allow their citizens time to pursue their dreams. Americans, on the other hand, are always chasing the "American Dream," which isn't really a dream so much as a shackling which prevents you from pursuing other, more gratifying dreams. The below discussion is a roadmap for removing those shackles and pursuing an alternative dream towards happiness.

countries is astounding. A typical private university in the United States costs approximately $33,500 per year, in tuition alone.[2] Including room and board, those costs can increase to $50,000-60,000/year. At a four-year university, that amounts to almost $200,000. Considering most Americans live paycheck to paycheck and are unable to save any substantial amount of money,[3] the fact that many of them choose to accumulate upwards of a quarter of a million dollars in debt for a college degree is astonishing. Even if you can pay off this debt in the amount of $10,000 per year (a staggering $833/month), it would take you twenty years to pay it off. And that doesn't even include interest, typically 7-10% unless you are able to get a government loan, and then it might be 3-5%.[4]

To make matters even worse, most people willingly accumulate this debt only to discover that at the end of their four years of college, they are unable to get a job. Or alternatively, the only job they are able to get is one that didn't require a college degree to begin with (e.g., service industry, retail etc.). In fact, in a recent study, 41% of college graduates were working jobs that didn't require a college degree.[5] Nevertheless, these unemployed graduates are still

---

[2] http://en.wikipedia.org/wiki/College_tuition_in_United_States.

[3] According to a recent study, 27% of Americans have no savings at all and 50% have less than a three-month cushion.
http://money.cnn.com/2013/06/24/pf/emergency-savings/index.html.

[4] The average American college student actually graduates with approximately $27,000 in debt
(http://money.cnn.com/2012/10/18/pf/college/student-loan-debt/index.html), but this figure is likely misleading because many students' parents assist them with their college tuition fees. As discussed further below, if these students would think more long-term, perhaps they'd go to a less expensive school and use their parents' extra money for something more meaningful later in life.

[5] https://www.insidehighered.com/quicktakes/2020/02/18/41-recent-grads-work-jobs-not-requiring-degree.

required to pay back all of their college debt, which they often can't afford to do, resulting in a lifetime of financial struggle.[6]

The alternative to a private university is a public or state one, which is still shockingly expensive compared to university costs in other countries, but is nevertheless about half the cost of a private college, or much less if you go to a community college as opposed to a major, accredited university. Compared to college tuition fees in other developed countries, however, America's tuition system is nothing short of ludicrous. For example, the average cost of yearly tuition in other first-world countries, for its own citizens, is as follows: Australia ($4,763); Canada ($4,939); Denmark (FREE); Finland (FREE); Germany (FREE); Italy ($1,658); Japan ($5,229); Netherlands ($2,420); Norway (FREE); Sweden (FREE).[7] What's even more astonishing is that many of these countries also offer free, or very nominal, tuition for foreign students.[8] While I'm not suggesting American students should flock oversees for their college education, it's at least something to consider when the alternative is accumulating years of debt and the prospect of not finding employment upon graduation.

For me, the decision to go to a public university (the U of I) was a no-brainer, for not only was it a very good school (and a renowned party school to boot), but since I knew I would have to pay for half of it (my parents offered to split it

---

[6] This book was written before Joe Biden's proposal to cancel up to $10,000 in student debt for certain income levels, a proposal that's currently still pending in the courts and also of questionable merit considering it asks non-indebted taxpayers to relieve debt agreed upon by other taxpayers under what essentially was an arm's length (i.e., fair) transaction.

[7] https://www.insider.com/cost-of-college-countries-around-the-world-2018-6.

[8] http://www.scholars4dev.com/4031/list-of-european-countries-with-tuition-freelow-tuition-universities-colleges/.

with me, mainly because of my choosing to go to a private high school), I wanted to take on as little debt as possible. This same thinking led me to stay at the U of I for law school, although this time I paid for it all on my own, fortunately being able to offset some of the cost by teaching a Public Speaking course to undergraduates during my second and third years of law school.

Time and time again, I'm amazed how many people attend these private universities, basically handicapping themselves for the rest of their lives. Even more shocking, and as addressed earlier when discussing my formidable high school years, is when kids decide to attend an inferior private school over a superior (and vastly cheaper) public school. Presumably because it's their parents' money and not theirs, but if they could stop and think long-term for just a moment, they'd probably realize they'd be far better served in the future by attending a state school and putting that extra money towards something far more meaningful in the future (e.g., a home, a car, or even their kids' future).

In fact, my ex-wife, who's from Ohio but attended the University of Maryland (a public school but since she was out-of-state she, or more aptly her parents, paid out-of-state tuition), often used to say that if she could do it again, she likely would have attended a public university in Ohio and asked her parents to put the extra money in a trust for her future. But at the time, in her understandably juvenile view, she thought that if her parents were paying, why wouldn't she take the opportunity to live somewhere else other than Ohio where she had spent her entire life up until then (and let me tell you folks, as described further below, Ohio ain't it). At the time, however, like so many others I imagine, she was unaware that whatever extra money her parents would have saved by sending her to an in-state rather than out-of-state school, would be hers later in life. Her parents likely didn't tell her that because they didn't want it to sway her decision (a justifiable reason). Fortunately for my ex, unlike most

Americans, she had the determination, intelligence, resources, and frankly luck to overcome this decision.

Another context in which I often saw this classic mistake arise is when I first started working at my first law firm. There were approximately thirty-five first-year associates when I began working there, and only a handful went to a public university. The vast majority went to private universities like the University of Chicago, Northwestern, Stanford (recall the nice partner in my annual review), Harvard, Yale, Georgetown, or even public universities like Michigan, but like my ex, they weren't from Michigan and so they paid out-of-state tuition. But at the end of the day, we were all making the same amount of money (approximately $160,000/year). The difference, however, was that I "only" graduated with approximately $50,000 in debt, whereas most of my colleagues graduated with upwards of $200,000 in debt. And almost unanimously, they all told me that if they could do it again, they would have done what I did (i.e., gone to the best public school they could get into which would allow them to achieve the same level of "success" they achieved by going to a private school). The result was that I was able to leave big firm law after only a few years (though I ultimately decided to stay longer to accumulate more wealth and also because I hadn't yet achieved personal happiness), whereas many of my colleagues felt compelled to stay for much longer, just so they could pay off their education debt, often at the expense of doing something they were truly passionate about.

In light of all of the foregoing, the lesson I would impart upon young people today is that if they choose to go to college, go to the best bang for your buck college you can get into, and to think more about the long-term financial impact of your decision, as opposed to the long-term social impact of it. In fact, the most prudent scenario might be to do what my younger brother did, which is go to a community/junior college for two years, where the cost is a fraction of a four-year university, and then transfer to a four-year university after two years. That way, you still get a degree from a four-year college but you only pay for two years of it. Nobody will ever know or even question the fact that you began at a community college, but you'll save two years of four-year college tuition by doing so.

More significantly, however, in light of the aforementioned astronomical costs associated with going to college, combined with the ease of starting a business online and other recent socio-economic factors, this is the first time in modern American history that going to college is no longer the automatic correct decision for most middle to upper class Americans. In many scenarios, it might make more sense for a high school graduate to forego college altogether and instead head straight into the workforce, or alternatively a trade school which is becoming increasingly popular. But whether you decide to go to college or not, the primary point here is that under no circumstance should you go into a lifetime of debt in order to do so, as the end result will be forever handicapping every major decision you will make for the rest of your life. As discussed earlier, an alternative for those who want a college education but can't afford one and don't want to accumulate massive debt in order to obtain one, might be to look overseas at schools which offer free tuition, even for international students.

And for those people who are fortunate enough to have their education paid for by their parents, I urge you not to choose the most expensive school just because you can, but rather, if you can work out an arrangement with your parents whereby whatever money they save by sending you to a cheaper college, they'll put into a trust fund for your use later in life, trust me, you'll be much better served down the road. Unless of course you plan on just living off of your parents for the rest of your life. But even then, circumstances change. And who knows, you may up needing that extra $100-200K that you wasted on an inferior (or similar) college, just because you could.[9]

Buying a Home (for non-investment purposes)

Similar to burdening yourself with a lifetime of college debt, many young professionals also burden themselves by buying a home well before they can really afford it. Unlike the burden of education debt, even I was unable to dodge this bullet. At the age of twenty-five, with only two years of work experience and approximately $100,000 in savings (not counting the approximate $50,000 I had accumulated in education debt), I decided to purchase a $380,000 condo in downtown Chicago. My reasoning was that I had just started my legal career and since I was only licensed to practice law in Illinois, it was a pretty safe bet that I would be in Chicago for the foreseeable future. After doing a lot of independent research, the general consensus was that if you planned to be in the same city for at least 3-4 years, it probably made more sense to buy than to rent, as the former allows you certain tax deductions (for real estate taxes and mortgage interest payments) and equity, whereas the latter offered you neither. So at the age of twenty-five, I put approximately $20,000 (or 1/5 of my life savings) into a condo, and also committed myself to a $360,000 mortgage (two mortgages in fact), to be paid back over the next thirty years.

Had it not been for two catastrophic events, my decision to buy instead of rent may not have been too hampering. But such is life I suppose. The first event, a personal one, came within a few months of when I bought my condo when I

---

[9] There are a few instances where I do think attending a private (or out-of-state), elite university might be worth it. For example, if you aspire a career in politics, or to be a federal judge, certain doors might be open to you by attending such elite/"prestigious" universities that might not otherwise be open to you if you don't.

realized I no longer wanted to work for my law firm. Fortunately, the job market was still good and so I was able to switch law firms without too much difficulty, but if that had happened a year or two later (or God forbid I had to move cities for a new job), I would have been in serious trouble. The second event occurred when the housing market collapsed within a year or so of my buying my condo. Suddenly, my $380,000 condo was now worth closer to $300,000. Again, fortunately I was committed to Chicago at the time and was able to afford my mortgage, so I was able to weather the storm. But if circumstances had been different, I could have been in serious trouble.

Fast forward five years later when my ex and I decided to move to New York, the housing market still hadn't picked up. That, combined with the fact that I wasn't sure how my move to NYC would go (both career-wise and moving in with my then girlfriend for the first time) led me to rent my place rather than sell it. Renting a property in and of itself is a hassle. Renting one while residing in another state (let alone country) is a whole different level of headache. Perhaps I just had bad luck and got a tenant from hell, but every month there would be some issue with the rent. Of course, I was still responsible for my monthly mortgage which was automatically deducted from my savings account, plus I was paying rent in NYC, which you may recall is not cheap. On top of the rent issues, I also received several violation notices from my condo board for infractions caused by my tenant. Like my mortgage, I of course was responsible for those as well.

But the real headache came when my ex and I decided to quit our jobs and travel/move to Asia. Because the housing market was still shit, and because I guess I was a glutton for punishment, I decided to try to continue renting my condo (albeit to a new tenant as mine thankfully did not want to renew her lease) rather than try to sell and take a substantial loss. After hiring an agent to assist with the rental process, who assured me my place (a very unique one in an excellent location with state of the art everything and excellent amenities) would rent in no time, after several showings, she quickly informed me that my tenant (actually a sub-tenant as my tenant had the audacity to sub-lease without my approval) was making it impossible for her to do her job by keeping the place in dire conditions (among other things like general filthiness, apparently the sub-tenant was a chef and would keep live seafood in the fridge for weeks at a time). Considering I'm anal retentive and OCD, you can only imagine how much this frustrated me. After several failed attempts to get him to clean up his act, and further threats to evict him (though in reality the eviction process in Illinois and generally is extremely arduous and expensive, and is setup to completely favor tenants over owners), I eventually decided I just wanted to sell the place, even if it meant taking a somewhat sizeable loss.

Very fortunately, shortly after coming to this conclusion, a neighbor of mine who was looking to buy a bigger condo in the same building (he owned a one bedroom whereas mine was two bedrooms) reached out to me to buy my place sans real estate brokers. Considering real estate brokers typically take a 3-5% commission, the $10,000-15,000 savings I'd be making by not using a broker made the deal too good to pass up. In the end, I still had to write a check for about $10,000 to get out of the deal (on top of the $20,000 down payment I put down five years earlier, which by this time, I had already considered a sunk cost), but it was well worth it. For as happy as I had been when I first bought the place, I was even happier to get rid of it. Owning real estate for personal use (as opposed to investment purposes) is literally crippling. Every decision you will make in life will be based around that property. Although it may cost more in the long-run to rent rather than buy (and even that is questionable, especially if the housing market collapses shortly after you buy like it did for me), the freedom you're afforded by renting is worth far more than any savings you'll realize from buying.

Although I'm all for buying properties for investment purposes (and have recently begun doing so and intend to continue doing so), in particular short-term rentals for cash flow purposes, I'll never buy another property for solely personal use again, at least not in the U.S. There are simply too many variables at play for such a big commitment (e.g., job, family, health, desire to remain in that city or even that part of the city, etc.). And all of those are personal factors. Perhaps the biggest factor of all is that if something catastrophic happens to your home, if you own it, you're financially (and legally) responsible, whereas if you rent, your landlord is the one on the hook for any loss. By way of example, my friend and her husband bought a huge five-bedroom house in the suburbs of Chicago years ago. Less than three months after they moved, a devastating storm flooded their entire basement, forcing them to evacuate and costing them tens of thousands of dollars in damage (both to the home itself and all of their personal possessions in the basement). Fortunately, they were both safe and I think their insurance might have paid for most or even all of the damage/repair, but barring insurance, they were on the hook for all of the loss, both to their home and their personal possessions. If they were renting, on the other hand, the landlord would have to repair the basement (a likely $10,000 cost in and of itself), and they'd only be out their personal possessions.[10]

---

[10] As a condo owner, the equivalent nightmare might be getting hit with what's called a "special assessment" (an assessment on top of your monthly assessment that is split between all of the condo owners in an association to fix/repair something, usually substantial). When I owned my condo in Chicago, I was hit with a $2,000 special assessment one year to fix/repair our balconies. Of course, I hadn't noticed anything wrong with my balcony, but when your condo association votes to do

For anyone considering buying a home, I strongly caution you to consider the commitment you're making. For most people, it will be the biggest financial commitment they will ever make, yet so many young people do it without even thinking twice. Most of my friends who bought condos in the city in their mid/late twenties have since sold them as they flocked to the suburbs. And many of them took a substantial financial loss. The less fortunate ones were forced to deal with the headache of renting because they were unable to afford the loss of selling.

So be warned, if you're deciding between renting and owning (again strictly for personal use and not investment purposes), opt on the much safer side of renting. In particular with today's high interest rates (7-8% instead of 3-4% as in previous recent years), recent studies have shown it's cheaper to rent than to buy in literally almost every major American city.[11] So unless you know with 100% certainty (and who really knows anything with 100% certainty) that you'll be living in the same city (and neighborhood) for the next 10 plus years, and able to afford your monthly mortgage even in the event of unemployment or a change in career, I'd advise you to rent. But if you do buy, buy modestly, unlike myself. When I bought my condo, I was debating between a one-bedroom and two-bedroom. I recall everyone telling me to go for the two-bedroom because it had better resale value. Of course, when the market crashed, nothing had resale value. Fortunately, I was able to rent out my 2nd bedroom to a good friend of mine for four of the five years I owned the place

---

something, you're obligated to comply. Similarly, shortly after buying a condo in Denver, I was hit with another sizeable special assessment, but at least my Denver condo I rent out half of the year and so while the assessment stung initially, ultimately the property still generates cash-flow for me on an annual basis.

[11]https://www.businessinsider.com/real-estate-renting-buying-affordability-mortgage-rates-home-prices-rent-2024-5.

(nowadays called house-hacking; who knew back then!!!). But for the other year, I probably lost over $10,000 and all I had to show for it was an empty bedroom, which of course I never used. So take note would-be home owners. And please heed my advice, or proceed at your own financial peril.

To conclude this section, as mentioned above, since initially writing this book, I've since bought a condo in Denver that I short-term rent approximately half the year and in that half the year it makes 2x my mortgage for the entire year. I also recently bought a 2nd home in Myrtle Beach, South Carolina that I also short-term rent approximately 8-9 months/year and live in for free the remaining few months. All told that property cash flows at approximately 10-15% plus the free usage. And then I own two other properties in rural Pennsylvania with a business partner which to date have had varying degrees of success.

In light of these successes and several friends who've had similar success, I plan to add to my real estate (in particular short-term rental) portfolio in the next few years (once interest rates inevitably come down again) and ultimately hope to own up to five homes that will pay for themselves, generate income for me and allow me free usage. However, there's a big difference between an investment property that generates cash flow (considered an asset on the balance sheet) and a home that you live in which generates no income (a liability on the balance sheet). This section was geared towards the latter.

In fact, I recently came across an interesting social media post that suggested that the "American Dream" was created by big banks and big corporations in order to get Americans to buy houses that would handcuff them to those cities and their employers for the rest of their lives. Viewing everything in totality, it's hard to argue against that.

Buying a Car and Other Life Necessities (e.g., Furniture, Clothes, Etc.)

After buying a home, a car is probably the second most expensive financial commitment a person will make in their life (other than perhaps an engagement ring or kids, the latter of which are far more financially committing but often not considered as such, though perhaps I'll dispel that theory later on). Regarding a car, depending on where you live, it may either be a necessity or a luxury. In Chicago, for example, if you live and work in the city, it's a luxury as public transportation can get you most places (though it's nowhere as good as say NYC, London, Tokyo, etc.). If you live and/or work in the suburbs, however, then it's probably a necessity. In NYC, on the other hand, a car is at best a luxury, and at worst an inconvenience, as the subway can take you pretty much anywhere you need to go (if you live in Long Island or another neighboring borough, however, then you may need a car to get to/from the closest train station or even into the city if you so choose).

If you decide that you do in fact need a car, then I urge you to buy a used, rather than new, one. A car is generally considered one of the poorest investments you can ever make. They say that a new car typically loses 20-30% of its value the moment it leaves the lot, with few exceptions (e.g., Jeep Wranglers I've heard tend to hold their value better than almost any other car). A used car, on the other hand, typically retains most of its value minus any depreciation for mileage and/or wear and tear. After driving a Nissan Altima with close to 100,000 miles for my last two years of law school (graciously given to me by my mom and stepdad as a college graduation present), upon beginning my career as a lawyer (particularly at one of the top firms in the city/world), I knew it was time for an upgrade. Like my father, I'm a sucker for fine automobiles. Unlike my father, however, who always wanted the newest toys/models, I was perfectly fine "settling" for a luxury automobile a few years old. My father, on the other hand, preferred to lease a car so he could always have the newest model. While there's merit behind that decision if you like having new toys every few years, for someone who struggles with money like my father did for most of his life, that was a poor financial decision.

When I purchased my first car, I spent several weeks searching the entire Midwest area for exactly what I was looking for (a two door Mercedes coup with grey/tan leather interior, blue exterior, and a sunroof). New, I knew these cars went for approximately $45,000. After a little research, however, I discovered I could get exactly what I was looking for, a few years old, with less than 30,000 miles, for about half the cost. The car was in Grand Rapids, Michigan however (about a 4-5 hour drive from Chicago), so one day after work, my stepdad picked me up and drove me to Michigan, and I returned home in my sweet new ride.

I had that car for about 5-6 years, and it treated me extremely well. It rarely broke down and when it did it only required minor repair. And even better, when I finally sold it upon moving to NYC, I was able to sell it for about $10,000, meaning I only spent about $15,000 on it over a 5-6 year span. Not bad for a Mercedes. The point is, unlike the decision between buying and renting a car, if you decide you need to have a car, you are far off better buying than renting, for unlike the housing market which fluctuates greatly, there is always a market for used cars, and that market remains relatively stable. Also, most dealerships allow you to trade in your car for a newer model (thereby offsetting the cost of your new car), whereas you can never trade in your home for a new model. Rather, with a home, you're frequently left trying to time your new home purchase with the sale of your previous home, for both practical purposes and also tax advantages (e.g., 1031 exchange) often leaving you tentatively "homeless" (i.e., living with family or friends or renting temporarily) or with two homes/mortgages for a few months or longer.

Similar to cars, when buying furniture or other life necessities (e.g., clothing, food, etc.), you should also consider buying used products, or at a minimum, discounted ones. Perhaps it's because my mom and stepdad spent the majority of their careers owning a direct mail coupon franchise (you know, those envelopes you get in the mail that contain numerous coupons for local businesses in your neighborhood, most of which may be of little use/interest to you but some of which you find very valuable--e.g., free delivery on a pizza, free appetizer from your favorite Chinese takeout, discounted dry cleaning, a free car wash, etc.), but from a very young age, I've always been taught why pay full price when you can get the same (or substantially similar) product/experience for less.

From Groupon, to Restaurant.com, to Living Social, to my parents' own direct mail coupons, I have always been an avid discount shopper. As a kid, my friends always called me the "coupon King," largely because of my parents' business.[12] My ex-wife was an equally avid saver. In fact, you may recall we bought our online TEFL course which prompted our RTW/move to Asia with a Groupon. The course typically costs $500-700 per person. We paid $70 each. When we lived in NYC for a year and a half, we had a date night every Wednesday wherein we'd go to a different neighborhood and check out a different restaurant. Because we were new to NYC, every restaurant was new to us. Consequently, we often chose our restaurant for date night based on what coupon site had the best deal/looked like the best restaurant. A typical $100 meal would end up costing us $50. Doing this

---

[12] Since my parents were in the coupon business, the result was that my entire childhood (and even into adulthood) I had an endless supply of gift certificates/credits/coupons to various restaurants, dry cleaners, car washes, clothing stores, gyms, tanning salons, etc. Thanks mom/stepdad!"

once (or sometimes twice) a week, we probably saved close to $5,000/year. These are just some of the examples of how we saved money on an everyday basis.

Even in Thailand, I was always amazed by the malls in Bangkok, particularly the Siam area. Specifically, I was amazed by all of the fancy designer stores (e.g., Gucci, Armani, Rolex, Chanel, Prada, Louis Vuitton, etc.) selling single items of clothing and accessories for hundreds or thousands of dollars. What's most amazing, however, is that directly across the street, at one of our favorite night markets, you could get substantially the same products for $5-10. Of course, people will tell you that they're fakes or knockoffs, but who really cares. If the issue is quality, even if the fake or knockoffs break, you can buy ten or twenty (or sometimes even a hundred) for the price of one genuine product. They certainly won't break that many times. If the issue is perception (i.e., what will people think of you if you wear fake clothing/jewelry), then you likely have bigger issues to deal with. Literally there's an expression that Louis Vuitton and Gucci have made millions off people going broke by trying to look rich.

Living in Thailand, my ex and I bought countless items from the local markets, and frankly, I can't think of a single item we ever paid retail for at a brand-name store where we could have gotten that same (or a substantially similar) item at a local market. From our work clothes which we bought entirely at the markets (my dress shirts cost on average $7-8 while my slacks I was able to find for a whopping $3 each in Phnom Penh, Cambodia; my ex's dresses and blouses cost typically $7-8; our shoes which we wore the entire year cost $5-15; and most amazingly, my ties were $1 each--compare the latter to a Hermes tie my good friend bought me as a gift in exchange for a personal favor I did for her--the tie retailed at about $200; great tie though/I still have/wear it:), to our electronics (we bought a Samsung tablet and Samsung smartphone at a notorious used/fake Bangkok electronics market for about 1/3 of what they typically retail for, and both worked relatively flawlessly while we were there, and when we did have an issue with my smartphone, the store we bought it from fixed it for no extra cost), to our appliances (e.g., iron, fans, hot water heater, blender, etc.) which we bought at the infamous "Thieves Market" in the Chinatown district of Bangkok, to everyday accessories (sunglasses and watches which we bought for $5 each, compared to the $100 and $2,500 pairs I respectively owned in the States, the former of which I've lost on several occasions and the latter of which my ex father-in-law and ex mother-in-law graciously gave me as an engagement present and I subsequently left behind in my mom's safety deposit box at her bank as there was no way I was taking it on a trip around the world), we literally saved thousands of dollars on everyday purchases.

In fact, at this point in my life, I can't ever fathom paying full price for anything ever again, at least not for products I know I can get for substantially cheaper somewhere else, even if they are fake/knockoffs or used. At the end of the day, they're all for personal use and they're all depreciable products, so why pay any more than you have to. I often akin it to the types of places my ex and I would stay at while we were traveling (often referred to as guesthouses or hostels). While others pay hundreds of dollars a night for their hotel, my ex and I, on average, paid about $15-20 per night. Sometimes that included free breakfast, air-conditioning, and hot water, but it always included free Wi-Fi (our only means of accessing the internet while traveling). In Vietnam and Cambodia we were paying as little as $5-10/night.

Our rationale was that we spent as little time as possible in our hotel room, so why spend any more than we had to. We'd much rather spend that money on an activity or even a meal, though the latter we typically only spent $5-10, as we almost always ate local meals when traveling. We never understood why people spend hundreds of dollars a night on accommodation when the only time they're in their room is when they're sleeping. If you like to hang out in your hotel I suppose it's a different story, but we were traveling in order to see a city or country, not that country's hotel amenities.

Typically, my ex and I would leave our hotel by 9 am and not return until after 10 pm, or later. Sometimes we'd come back in the afternoon to shower/change, but that's it. So on average, we were probably in our hotel room for 1-2 hours per day when weren't sleeping. To me, this hardly seemed to justify spending hundreds of dollars per night when you can spend as little as $15-20. Perhaps there are certain, special occasions which call for a fancy hotel room (e.g., a honeymoon, anniversary, or an occasion where you literally want to spend the entire time in your hotel room or at your hotel, and thus in essence your activity is your hotel, such as the Maldives from what I hear), but as a general rule, we tried to spend as little as possible on accommodation while traveling, and we often felt as though as we got just as much bang for our buck as people who spent hundreds of dollars a night.

A classic example of this is when our parents came to visit us in Thailand. It was the only time during our travels when we stayed at nice hotels as they were kind enough to put us up at their hotel. And while the experiences were wonderful and we were extremely grateful for their generosity (and also to spend the additional time with them), in our view, it just wasn't worth the extra cost. For example, spending $200 a night on a hotel could equate to 10 nights' worth of a hotel for me and my ex. Multiply that times five, and my ex and I could travel for 50 days as opposed to five days, for essentially the same cost. I suppose when you take a typical American vacation which equates to only 10-15 days a year, you can afford to spend $200/night on accommodation (and in fact that's likely why most Americans do spend that amount because they can only take so many vacation days). But if you're considering the alternative lifestyle that my ex

109

and I chose, know that you can travel for approximately 50 days for the same amount you would typically spend on a 5-10 day vacation, and at very little sacrifice.[13]

In fact, my favorite exemplary story regarding this issue while traveling with our parents is when the hotels we stayed at with our parents didn't even provide free internet. Typically, when we traveled, the #1 thing we looked for in a hotel is good (and free) internet. Almost all backpacker hotels offer free internet. Most of them provide it in every room, some only in the lobby/common area. But none of them ever have the audacity to try to charge for it (for if they did, they'd surely be out of business in no time). At a hotel we stayed at in Singapore with my ex's mom, however, they had the nerve to try to charge her $80 per day for internet use. $80 per day!!! That alone would be four nights' accommodation (with free internet) at most places in SE Asia (granted Singapore is not like anywhere else in SE Asia, or even the world for that matter; e.g., a liter of Smirnoff vodka which retails for $20 in most cities cost $110 at a 7-11 in Singapore, at least when we were there in 2014ish).[14] Anyways, when we alerted my ex's mom to this little factoid,

---

[13] Even nowadays when I travel approximately 3-6 months/year, my places in Denver and Myrtle Beach typically rent out for $200-350/night depending on the time of year, and I spend approximately $75-100/night which is what allows me to travel so much without dipping into my savings, and in fact, still generate income from my two homes which double as vacation homes for typical Americans who are willing/able to pay higher amounts since they only vacation two weeks a year. But I will almost never spend more than $100/night on accommodation, even if it means sleeping in hostel dorm rooms which I still do on very rare occasion, most often in fancy ski towns where a dorm bed is literally $100/night (e.g., Whistler, Aspen/Vail).

[14] Incidentally this is one of the several reasons I do not like Singapore. It's like if Dubai (which granted I haven't been to but have heard enough about) moved to SE Asia. What gave them the right to setup shop in the cheapest part of the world and literally charge the highest prices. The nerve of them!!!

she was successfully able to negotiate "free" internet ("free" being a loose term as the room we stayed in was approximately $200/night).

Anyways, the point of all of this, and a point I tried to touch upon earlier in this book, is why pay any more than you have to when you can have the same (or substantially similar) experience or product for less. Sure, there are certain special occasions when splurging for the best or genuine experience/product is worth the extra cost. But as a general rule, why spend any more than you have to, especially on items/activities with limited time value (e.g., hotel rooms, restaurants to a certain degree, depreciable items like cars, clothes, accessories, etc.). Taken individually, it may not seem like you're saving much. But collectively, over time, trust me, it adds up. And if you're like me and my ex, perhaps you can translate that into an extended vacation, rather than a typical 1-2-week American holiday. Or even better, invest that extra money you save into a cash-flowing asset like a short-term rental that pays for your lifestyle and allows you to retire early like me and pursue your personal passions, rather than work an additional twenty years.

Marriage

Marriage is a funny thing. It marks the union of two people. In theory, it's supposed to last for the rest of your life. In reality, it often only lasts for a few years (mine lasted five, though as previously alluded to and discussed further below, compared to an average American couple in terms of time spent in each other's physical presence, more like 25-30 years), and many people get married several or more times over the course of their life. Inherent in the concept of marriage are several hallmark traditions which take place in the months (or sometimes years) leading up to the marriage. All of these traditions are widely accepted (and embraced) by most Americans, particularly the middle to upper class ones.

They are all intended to celebrate the would be couple as they begin their journey in life together. Yet each of them costs an exorbitant amount of money, money which could be put to far better use to help the married couple start their life together, or later in life.

But instead, vast sums are spent on mostly materialistic, impracticable things that provide no real tangible benefit to the married couple. The result is that married couples often spend their lives crippled in financial debt, when if they had just been a little more prudent and practical upon getting married, their married lives could be far better off. Particularly when you consider that one of the leading causes of divorce is financial problems, it's shocking that these traditions continue to exist today, and moreover, that Americans embrace them wholeheartedly, perhaps now more than ever.

The Engagement Ring

The greatest marketing strategy/scam in the history of consumer products (besides perhaps the aforementioned "American Dream" of buying a home) was created by De Beers in the mid-1900s. The concept of a dower (aka bride price) goes back thousands of years before, but De Beers was able to turn the traditional concept of a dower (e.g., the would-be groom offering a goat, a cow or just plain old money to the wife or the wife's family in exchange for taking her hand in marriage) into a money-making machine that would last generation after generation. The concept was simple: if you want to show your future bride how much she means to you, buy her the biggest piece of jewelry (often a diamond) you can afford. The bigger (aka more expensive)

---

[15]   thejimenezlawfirm.com/what-percent-of-marriages-end-in-divorce-because-of-money/.

the diamond, the more you loved her. After all, as De Beers proclaimed, "diamonds are forever."

This single marketing ploy and accompanying tagline has led generations of men into a dick pissing contest (i.e., my penis/net worth is bigger than yours), and in turn, has led woman after woman to gloat amongst her friends and family that her soon to be husband loves her more (and has more money) than everyone else's. The general rule of thumb for any self-respecting man these days is that you should spend approximately three months of your salary on an engagement ring for your prospective bride. THREE MONTHS OF YOUR SALARY! Considering most people in America already live paycheck to paycheck as it is, spending three months of your salary on anything, let alone a piece of jewelry that has no tangible benefit, is simply ludicrous.

Let's think about this rationally for a second. When a man proposes to a woman, he is basically saying, I want to spend the rest of my life with you. A life that, in theory, you will be building together. Yet, almost without fail, American men (and women who are equally if not even more culpable) believe the best way to start their lives together is by spending more than you've ever spent in your entire life in a single purchase on a single piece of jewelry, just to show your future bride how much you love her. Putting aside all of your preconceived notions about this issue, surely you must admit, it sounds insane. Basically, what you're saying, is that you love your future wife so much that you're willing to sacrifice your entire financial future together, just so she knows how much you love her (and to be more frank, just so she can show all of her friends and family how much money you have, or at least *had*).

A couple of caveats for the naysayers here. First, for those who say that diamonds don't really lose their value and so they're always a good investment, that may be so, but surely they're not as good of an investment as say, a CD, ETF/mutual fund, a house, or just a plain old money market account. Like any product, once used, they depreciate over time. Not to mention the risk of damage or theft, which often leads people to purchase insurance, which merely adds to the expense. Second, for those who say "Well, if times get tough, they can always just sell the diamond," though this may be true, let me ask you, do you know a single couple that sold their diamond engagement ring because they needed the cash? Likely not. Rather, an engagement ring often gets passed down from generation to generation, many times just sitting idle in a safety deposit box for years waiting for the next would-be bride to come along. In fact, the only time an engagement ring is typically sold is upon divorce or a break-up of the engagement. So arguing that it can often be liquidated if needed is not really a good argument, because in reality that rarely happens.

So why then has this tradition persisted for generation after generation? Undoubtedly one of the biggest reasons is because it has now become a source of bragging, for both the bride and the groom. How many times have you heard someone say "Oh my god, did you see the size of her ring? Her fiancé must be loaded." Or how many times have you seen a newly engaged woman posing for a photo with her ring finger prominently displayed. In a less vein world, that former expression should be changed to "Oh my god, did you see the size of her ring? Her fiancé must be stupid." Putting bragging and vanity aside, the only legitimate reason left for this tradition is to conserve the traditional notion of the dower. Though the tradition of a dower is somewhat antiquated, legitimate arguments can still be made for why a man should have to make a large, personal financial sacrifice before earning the right to take a woman's hand in marriage (e.g., to prove he can afford to take care of her, to compensate her for the opportunity cost of being courted by other prospective suitors, etc.). But for the life of me, I cannot comprehend why that sacrifice should come at the expense of both him *and* his future wife.

Instead of spending three months of your salary on a materialistic piece of jewelry that will provide no tangible benefit to you or your wife for the rest of your lives, why not take that money and put it towards something that will provide value: a car, a down payment on a house, your kid's future college education, even a trust fund for your wife in the event your marriage fails and she finds herself in need of money. Any of those things will provide far more benefit later in your life, the life you're supposedly building together, than a silly piece of jewelry.

For me and my ex-wife, though we had talked about it beforehand and she had professed to me from day one that she had never wanted a diamond engagement ring, for she too thought the entire concept was ridiculous, our choice was clear. Seeing as how we were about to embark on a trip around the world, we decided that rather than my buying her a fancy engagement ring that in reality would just sit in a safety deposit box for the indefinite future (as we clearly weren't going to travel around the world with an expensive diamond ring, just like I wasn't going to take the very expensive and generous watch her parents bought for me when I proposed to her), I would spend that money by paying for her portion of the trip, surely something that would provide a lifetime's worth of memories more than any piece of jewelry could. She, of course, was completely on board (pun intended) with the plan.

Two stories about our engagement ring situation confirmed both the brilliance and practicality of our plan, and also the fact that the majority of Americans will likely never embrace it. The first was when my ex and I went ring shopping in Columbus, OH (her hometown). Though we had already discussed our plan of buying her a modest engagement ring that she could wear around the world (I had also promised to buy her a much fancier ring upon returning to the U.S., if she so wished, but deep down I knew that simply wasn't her style), upon entering the jewelry store and perusing the simple gold and silver wedding bands, the woman who was helping us, unsurprisingly, suggested why not also look at the diamond rings. In response, we told her that rather than buying my ex an expensive engagement ring that she would likely never wear (and certainly not wear for the foreseeable future), we were planning to use that money on a bucket-list trip around the world for 3-4 months (literally Machu Picchu, the Amazon, the Taj Mahal, Mt. Everest and Ankor Wat, just to name a few). I'll never forget the look on that woman's face. Utter shock, and jealousy. And her response: "Wow. That's so much better than a diamond ring."[16]

The second story I recall which relates to this issue is when my ex and I started telling her friends of our grand plans right after we got engaged. Needless to say, all of them were insanely jealous, and one of them actually said, "I wish my boyfriend [of many years] would take me on a trip around the world."

My ex replied, "Well he can. Just tell him that when he eventually proposes, instead of spending 10-30K on an engagement ring, to just put that money towards a trip around the world."

---

[16] Incidentally, there was another gentleman (actually a kid probably about twenty-two years old) also in the store ring shopping that day (without his future fiancé). I vividly recall him perusing all of the diamond rings and several times telling the woman who was helping him that a certain ring was out of his price range. I could no doubt tell that he was pretty much spending his entire life savings (and likely borrowing money as well) on an engagement ring. I so badly wanted to tell him to save his money and instead spend it on something much more meaningful and tangibly beneficial. I wanted to tell him that if his fiancé to be really loved him and really wanted to spend her life with him, then she too would agree it would be ludicrous to spend his entire life savings on a piece of jewelry, when no doubt, money would be a constant struggle throughout their lives together. Of course, I didn't say any of this to him. I sure hope they're still together, and don't regret mortgaging their future on a silly piece of jewelry.

Her response, also unsurprisingly, was, "Oh no. There's no way I would give up that ring."

You see, that's the problem with America. Granted, most of my ex's friends are from NYC, very well off, and some or most would likely be considered JAPs (Jewish American Princesses – who are known to be the worst when it comes to vanity and their desire for material possessions), the disease is nevertheless endemic throughout America.[17] Frankly, I'm not sure if these women actually want the ring, or rather, if they just want to be able to show it off to their friends to prove to them (and themselves) how much money their fiancé has and how much he "loves" them.

Either way, looking at it rationally, there's no way you can argue against the notion that young American couples would be *far* better off if they started their lives together by putting whatever ridiculous amount of money the man is planning to spend on an engagement ring towards something much more meaningful and beneficial. As suggested earlier, a car, a down payment on a house, a CD/ETF, a trust fund for their future children, even a trust fund solely for the wife's benefit in the event of divorce. Anything would be better than a piece of jewelry that will provide no tangible benefit at any point in their life (unless they sell it for much less later in life which as discussed above rarely actually happens).

But sadly, my suspicion is that nothing will change. For Americans are far too egotistical, vein, jealous and in search of status symbols to think about the big picture. And consequently, the only ones to benefit from all of this are those

---

[17] As you may recall from earlier, one of the reasons that my ex moved to Chicago after graduation (where she knew almost no one) as opposed to NYC (where she had tons of family and friends) is because she didn't want to get caught up in the Jappy NYC scene that she knew so many of her friends would be a part of. Instead, she wanted to move to a new, Midwestern city and choose her own, less flashy/vein scene. Not coincidentally, that's one of the many reasons I married her.

in the diamond industry. As the saying from one of my favorite movies (The Usual Suspects) goes, "the greatest trick the devil ever pulled was convincing the world that he didn't exist." Well, I propose that the greatest trick ever pulled on the American people was by De Beers when they somehow convinced young Americans in love that the best way to start their future together was to spend their entire life savings on a product they were selling that would provide zero tangible benefit whatsoever to them at any point in their lives. The fact that it worked is remarkable. The fact that it's sustained itself for over fifty years is even more amazing. Suffice to say, whoever came up with that slogan is a pure (and very rich) genius.

The Wedding

Like the engagement ring, the traditional American wedding has become a phenomenon over time, similarly crippling and handicapping couples (and their parents) financially for years to follow. On average, Americans in big cities like New York spend upwards of $65,000 on a wedding that lasts A SINGLE NIGHT.[18] And this is the *average* cost of a wedding for the *average* American living in New York. For middle to upper class Americans, that figure is likely closer to $75,000-$100,000, and for wealthy Jewish people in Chicago and New York I've been told they often spend upwards of $200,000 on a wedding.[19] Unlike an engagement ring, which at least retains some value upon purchase, money spent on a wedding becomes completely obsolete upon completion of the wedding. All that's left are memories, some pictures

---

[18]   https://www.theknot.com/content/wedding-data-insights/real-weddings-study.

[19] The average cost of a wedding nationwide, irrespective of city or social class, is still a staggering $28,000. https://www.creditkarma.com/advice/i/unexpected-wedding-costs.

(though those cost extra when a professional photographer is used, which is almost always the case), and maybe some cake and other baked goods which have a short shelf life.

Once again, let's think about this rationally. If the average American is able to save $1,000/month, which is probably a generously high estimate, to pay for a $50,000 wedding (a modest wedding for any "self-respecting" middle to upper class bride), it would take a little over four years of saving. ALL FOR A SINGLE NIGHT. For a $75,000 wedding, it would take over six years of saving. And for a $100,000 wedding (not atypical for any big wedding in a major city on a Saturday night, particularly a JAP), it would take over eight years of saving. Considering that approximately 50% of marriages end in divorce,[20] and that the *average* divorced couple gets divorced in approximately eight years,[21] for many weddings, this means the couple will get divorced well before the wedding is even paid off.

Why then, do Americans have this tradition of having huge, expensive weddings to celebrate marriage?[22] For the same reason that men buy their prospective wives fancy expensive rings prior to proposing marriage: vanity, egotism, jealousy and other vices. They do it so that they can invite everyone they know (not just close family and good friends, but distant family and tangential friends) so they can show them what a wonderful husband their daughter (after all, traditionally, it is the father of the bride who pays for the

---

[20] https://www.wf-lawyers.com/divorce-statistics-and-facts/.

[21] http://www.families.com/blog/average-length-of-marriages.

[22] Similar to weddings, Jewish people also frequently throw extravagant bar and bat mitzvah parties when their children are approximately thirteen years old. These parties, like weddings, can typically cost upwards of $50,000-100,000, all for a single night's entertainment. Although the children often get thousands of dollars in gifts/money, like weddings, the return is hardly worth the investment. Yet, like an extravagant wedding, a bar or bat mitzvah party is often considered a right of passage for most middle to upper class American Jews.

wedding) has found, and so they can show everyone how proud of her they are and how much they love her.

Like the engagement ring, let me propose this: if parents were really proud of their daughter and wanted to show her how much they loved her, wouldn't they (and their daughter) be far better off if they spent a fraction of what a typical huge wedding costs and instead put the remaining amount towards their future in the form of a car, down payment on a house, trust fund for their future children, etc.? Instead of inviting 150-250 people, consisting primarily of distant relatives and tangential friends, why not just invite close family and good friends, the ones who *really* love them. And instead of having the wedding at a fancy hotel on a Saturday night, why not have it at their house, or if that isn't big enough, a favorite local restaurant. And instead of having it catered by an expensive caterer, why not cook your own food or order in from one of your favorite local restaurants. And instead of hiring a professional photographer, why not ask one of those distant relatives or tangential friends, who really shouldn't have been invited in the first place, to take pictures. They'll be honored just to have been invited. The list is endless. You get the idea.

For me and my ex, that's exactly what we did. Don't get me wrong, when we first discussed our impending marriage with her parents, as expected, they graciously wanted to throw us a huge, fancy wedding, the wedding of her (and any) daughter's dreams. And at first, we gladly accepted. But then we started thinking. Here we were, about to embark on a journey of ten thousand lifetimes, with no return date in sight, and in order to accomplish this feat, we were selling off literally everything we owned, minus our clothing and some other personal possessions. But we sold my condo, my car, our bicycles, our computers, and all of our furniture, both in our NYC apartment and in my Chicago condo.

So whenever we presumably returned to the US, we would need to repurchase all of these "essential" life possessions.

This would cost us tens of thousands of dollars. After already having spent tens of thousands of dollars on our many travels. So after thinking about it, we decided that rather than having a huge fancy wedding that would cost my ex's parents $50,000-100,000, we would rather have a small, intimate wedding, with only our closest friends and family, and when we eventually did return to the U.S., perhaps her parents could use some of the money they saved on our wedding to help us get back on our feet (e.g., help us buy furniture, a car, etc.). Being the practical and overly generous people that they are, not surprisingly, her parents were completely on board with our new plan.[23]

---

[23] In reality, our original plan was to have a small, intimate wedding at her parents' house in OH before we left for our RTW 1.0 (recall her parents strongly requested we get married before we left the States, to which we gladly agreed and also concurred it was the right decision), and then have a much bigger, more typical wedding at their house in AZ when we returned to the US in the summer of 2015. In fact, we even went so far as to put a down payment on the country club at her parents' home in AZ for Memorial Day weekend 2015. But then, after thinking about it further, we decided we would be far better off just having the smaller wedding in OH and then having her parents use that extra money to help us get back on our feet upon our return to the States. We also realized that a second, unofficial wedding, two years after our original, official marriage seemed a bit silly. Finally, though we didn't tell her parents this, we didn't want to be committed to returning to the U.S. on any specific date. Fortunately, her parents' country club agreed to refund her parents' down payment (or at least to give them a credit they could use towards golf, which they often play), but not without a strongly worded legal letter from yours truly reminding them of their legal duty under AZ law to mitigate their damages caused by our anticipatory breach of contract. I told them that I trusted they could find a replacement event for Memorial Day weekend (one of the most popular weekends of the year to get married in the U.S.) two years in advance. Considering the cancellation provision of their contract spelled out the consequences of canceling within 30, 60 and 90 days (but nothing further out), I told them I assumed two years was more than enough notice.

So that's exactly what we did. We had our wedding at her parents' house in Columbus, OH, in their beautiful and spacious backyard. We had about 100 guests consisting of our closest family and friends. Her mom graciously and heroically (because she only had a few months to plan it, whereas the typical American wedding is planned 9-12 months in advance, if not more) planned it. My ex and I had final sign-off on all of the major components (the rabbi, the food, the alcohol), but generally speaking, her mom planned everything in a simple, modest, yet remarkable fashion. In fact, everyone who attended the wedding had pretty much the same reaction: it was the most beautiful wedding they had ever been to. Much more beautiful than the typical huge hotel wedding, which costs 2-3 (or more) times as much.

As my ex pointed out, unlike most huge weddings where you typically only get to talk to the bride and groom for 2-3 minutes (usually during the obligatory round they make at dinner, stopping at each table for a few minutes to say hello and take a picture), at our wedding, we hung out with each of our guests the entire night. My ex was even giving my friends a tour of her childhood bedroom throughout the night. And that, more than anything we think, made our wedding more special than most (not to mention the weather gods couldn't have been more cooperative, providing a beautiful May day and evening outside in her parents' backyard, with ample green space and a beautiful pond to boot).

In addition to our modest wedding, both of our parents threw engagement parties for us, one in Chicago for my family and friends who couldn't make it to Ohio for the wedding, and another in NYC for her family and friends. Both of our engagement parties were at our house (the one in Chicago at my parents' and the one in NYC at mine and my ex's apartment), and we served deep dish pizza and deli sandwiches (albeit from Lou Malnotti's and 2nd Avenue Deli; we may be modest but we were still foodies), respectively.

The point of all of this is that, like an engagement ring, Americans typically spend extraordinary sums on weddings, often at the financial expense of the bride and groom's (and parents') future. In fact, I often hear stories of fathers having to work 5-10 extra years just to pay for their daughter's wedding. If Americans could step back and out of their egotistical shells for just a moment, I think they might realize what a waste of money (not to mention time; up to a year of planning) all of this is. And the irony is that these typical huge weddings often cause tons of family drama, often breaking the very bonds they are meant to forge. All so you can please and impress people that you aren't even really close to or friends with. Moreover, as our wedding proved, a smaller, intimate wedding is likely to be far more impactful and meaningful. So before you spend a year of your life and 5-10 years' worth of savings for a single night of entertainment, consider whether your time and money might be put to better use, which will likely result in more impactful memories anyways. Before concluding this section, two anecdotal stories may help further illustrate this point.

The first involves my good friend Samantha and her husband Tom.[24] Samantha is one of the sweetest girls you will ever meet. She is one of those girls that seems like she belongs in a Hollywood Disney movie, as the princess. She is always bubbly and happy. Her husband, Tom, is also a very nice guy. A little hard to get to know, but once he lets you in, he's as good of a man as they come. Samantha and Tom also happen to be two of the most beautiful people you'll ever meet. Whenever they take pictures together, you swear they belong in a GQ magazine or model photo shoot.

Anyways, Samantha and Tom got married years ago. I was fortunate enough to be asked to be an usher at their wedding. I gladly accepted. Their wedding was beautiful. Granted it

---

[24] Names have been changed for confidential/privacy purposes.

was a somewhat typical downtown Chicago hotel wedding on a Saturday night, but it was beautiful nonetheless. A couple of years after their wedding, I received a phone call from Samantha asking for some legal advice. Apparently, Tom's parents had contributed approximately $10,000 towards their wedding (their wedding as a whole probably cost between $50,000-75,000, if not more, and I believe Samantha's parents paid the rest), and I guess things didn't go exactly how they had wished (why I know not for as I said the wedding was beautiful and went off seamlessly), and now they wanted their money back. Of course, Samantha and Tom had already spent the money (on the wedding) so they were not inclined to give it back. But Tom's parents were so adamant that they went so far as to hire a lawyer who wrote Samantha and Tom a demand letter.

Samantha, in turn, requested that I help them write a response. Being the good friends that they were, I agreed, and even went so far as to get my law firm's approval to take on the case pro bono (aka for free). In my view, the case was simple: Tom's parents' gave Samantha and Tom an unconditional gift which therefore could not be revoked. I wrote their lawyer a response to that effect and also scolded her for fostering a client's behavior which was likely to lead to the demise of a family relationship, all for a relatively small amount. To my surprise and dismay, their lawyer wrote me back saying that the gift was conditioned on certain aspects of the wedding being tailored to her clients' liking, aspects that never came to fruition, and further, that Tom offered to give the money back at one point. And she had the text messages to prove it. Needless to say, my friends/"clients" neglected to inform me of those pivotal facts when I agreed to take their case pro bono.

In the end, after much deliberation, Samantha and Tom decided to give his parents their money back, and in doing so, they essentially cut ties with them indefinitely. It was a very sad ending to a very sad situation. And to think, this all resulted from what was supposed to be a beautiful and memorable occasion. The point is, big weddings can cause big headaches. It's actually not that surprising. Whenever so much money is involved, people have strong opinions about how it should be spent. For my friends Samantha and Tom, the result is that they now, at least last I heard, they have no contact with Tom's parents. Granted, maybe it's all for the better considering what type of parents would do such a thing, but it's still a very sad situation. And even more sad, I don't think it's that atypical of other situations. So rather than spending tens of thousands of dollars on a wedding that will last a single night and may ultimately lead to more unhappiness than happiness, why not have a more modest wedding and save everyone a lot of money and grief.[25]

The second story which illustrates the lunacy of big weddings involves my buddy Eric and his wife Heather. Eric and Heather are two of a kind. They are both very vibrant, outspoken and brash. While they both have huge hearts, I think sometimes they let their hearts get the better of their brains. Their wedding was a case in point. Although I regrettably couldn't attend as I was living in Thailand at the time, they had their wedding in a notorious US glamour/party city. From what I heard, their wedding spared no expense (not that anyone can spare expense in that city). The hotel alone which they and most of their guests stayed at cost approximately $500/night.

While I'm sure their wedding was beautiful and unforgettable, it came at a huge expense (both literally and figuratively). I know from personal experience that Eric was struggling with money at the time and had recently been laid

---

[25] As a further aside, years later Samantha told me that Tom was an unfortunate casualty of a Covid layoff and with two young kids in tow, money was tight. While she didn't say it, I wonder whether she would have reconsidered having that extravagant (albeit lovely) wedding which only lasted a single night.

off (in fact he actually asked me to borrow money a few years earlier to prevent his home from being foreclosed, which I was considering until his wealthy father stepped in to save the day, I believe). Yet, they somehow felt the need to throw a lavish wedding in an extravagant city, inviting everyone under the sun to help them celebrate their marriage. Though I'm sure it was the best night of their life (and again, personally, I was terribly sad to miss it), I also wonder whether they'll live to regret it in years to come.

Although they likely received financial assistance from their parents, in my view, I think they would have been far better off having a much smaller wedding and using whatever money they saved by not having a big wedding, on a honeymoon, or even something more beneficial like future mortgage payments (Eric has a very nice, but also very big, house) or a nest egg for further rainy days. But like most Americans, Eric and Heather only looked at the then and now. I sincerely hope that their shortsightedness doesn't come back to hurt them. And frankly, even if it does, I think they'll ultimately be okay as like I said Eric's father is very wealthy, but other Americans who make the same decisions aren't as fortunate.

So like the engagement ring, I caution any young person looking to get married to question the long-standing American tradition of having a huge, fancy wedding with tons of people you barely know. Rather, try to think of the big picture, and realize that the main purpose of a wedding is to celebrate love with the ones you love most. You don't need a lavish party to do that. All you need is your loved ones, some good food and perhaps some booze. Though the memories of your wedding will last a lifetime, the actual event will last only one night. Before spending 5-10 years of your savings for that night, think about what other uses that money could be put towards, all while maintaining the same lasting memories, perhaps even better.

Wedding Gifts/Honeyfund

After the engagement ring and wedding, the 3rd in the trifecta of mystifying American traditions when it comes to weddings is the concept of wedding gifts. Typically, when couples get married, they register at several popular, brand-name stores for all sorts of household items. From bedding and kitchenware at Bed Bath & Beyond, to kitchen appliances and dining room needs at Crate and Barrel, to all sorts of household items at places like Macy's, Nordstrom's, William & Sonoma, etc.

When registering, couples typically list how many items of each they "need," and then guests of the wedding can shop online for anything from a single, expensive item to several smaller items. Often times, before the couple is even married, they've accumulated tens of thousands of dollars in household goods.

I've never understood this tradition. Here's my question/issue with it: when couples get married, are they homeless beforehand? Are they lacking the basic necessities of life that they most often seem to register for (e.g., cutlery, bedding linen, dishes, etc.)? To the contrary, I would assume that since there are two people getting married, they should now have double of everything, particularly if the couple hasn't lived together before marriage.[26]

Critics of my viewpoint might argue that perhaps the couple already has the basic necessities of life, but they just

---

[26] Someone actually recently explained this bizarre phenomenon to me. Wedding registries were originally created generations ago, when the typical age for marriage was much younger and consequently the bride and groom often lived with their parents meaning they actually didn't own much of anything for themselves. Fast forward to today, however, when the typical age of marriage is much later and consequently the bride and groom often each have their own apartment/home filled with all of life's necessities, and the continued merit of a wedding registry strains serious credibility.

want nicer things, or things they've chosen together. My response, in addition to pointing out the obvious superfluous, materialistic, possession-accumulating American culture that fosters such behavior, is, do the couples really need other people to buy those things for them, or can't they just buy them for themselves? Personally speaking, when I was working in corporate America, if there was something I wanted that was of modest expense (i.e., not a car or $2,000 suit), I would just go out and buy it. I didn't need to wait around for a special occasion like marriage so I could ask my friends/family to buy me a Cuisinart. Just buy the damn Cuisinart!

The second typical response to my criticism is that what couples really want is money, but they can't just come right out and ask for money, so instead they "register" for certain items that they don't really need, but may want, solely in order to appease their guests. If this is in fact the case, then it's a pretty sad situation. If the people you're inviting to your wedding truly are your closest friends and family, then they should understand what you really want is money, and they should have no difficulty just giving you whatever amount of money they would have spent on one (or more) of your unnecessary registry gifts. And if they aren't truly your close friends and family, well, then you shouldn't have invited them to your wedding to begin with.

Putting that issue aside, however, there are many ways to appease your wedding guests over the gift situation, other than registering for silly, superfluous items that you don't really need. For example, my wife came up with two alternatives that I would strongly encourage others to consider. First, because we love to travel and knew we'd be doing a ton of traveling in the next several years, instead of registering for typical household items which we not only didn't need but in fact were in the midst of fire-selling, we registered for United Airlines dollars (unlike miles, the dollars we could use just like a gift card without any blackout dates, restrictions, expirations, etc.). Within the first few weeks of registering, the idea was such a hit that we accumulated over $2,000 in United Airlines funds and had to cut the registry off and think of other clever ways to register for things we actually needed in life.

The second clever idea that my ex came up with is to use what's called a honeyfund (honeyfund.com). A honeyfund basically allows you to register for whatever you want. It was originally created so couples could register for activities during their honeymoon (e.g., sunset dinner cruise, couples massage, even your hotel room, etc.). In reality, however, you can personalize it to register for literally whatever you want. But instead of your wedding guests making the purchases themselves, they simply put their credit card into the website, and your account/honeyfund is credited (in real US dollars) whatever amount they choose to spend. You can then withdraw the money whenever you want (or transfer it to your personal checking/savings account) and either spend it on the things that you registered for, or spend it however you want (or not spend it at all).

Because we knew we'd be traveling for three months over the summer immediately following our wedding, we decided to "register" for all of the activities and other expenses we'd be doing/incurring over the course of the trip. For example, we "registered" for our 4 day/3 night Machu Picchu trek, our three-night Amazon jungle adventure, our Iguazu Falls visit, our wine tour in Mendoza, Argentina, skiing in the Andes Mountains, our tour of the Taj Mahal, and most significantly, our eleven day EBC trek. In addition, we also "registered" for many of our individual flights throughout our trip, as well as several long bus rides. Like a typical registry, we divided the denominations of each gift such that people could give as little or as much as they wanted.

And like the United Airlines registry, the honeyfund registry was a huge success. All told, we received over $20,000 in gifts. Of course, in reality, as mentioned earlier, we (or I) had already paid for most of these activities in lieu of my ex's engagement ring, but our guests felt as though they were directly contributing to our RTW 1.0. In fact, when we finally embarked on our RTW 1.0, each time we'd do something that was on our honeyfund, we'd make a Facebook post about it and then tag the person(s) who contributed to the gift, thanking them for their generosity and support (of course, we also wrote traditional thank you cards before we left the States). Our honeyfund was such a success that we actually had to register for things we were doing on our RTW 2.0 (e.g., Halong Bay overnight boat cruise in Vietnam, trekking in the Philippine rice terraces, hiking volcanoes in Indonesia, scuba diving in Bali, etc.). The result was that we were still thanking people for their wedding gifts over a year after our wedding. To think, some people can't even afford to take a honeymoon because they (foolishly, in my opinion), spent all of their money on an engagement ring and/or wedding, and here my ex and I were, over a year after our marriage and still on our honeymoon.

And best of all, despite all of our travels (approximately thirty countries in over four years), we never even really dipped into our personal savings. In fact, after six months of traveling (plus countless weekend trips in Thailand), at the time of this initial writing, we still had over $13,000 left in our honeyfund. Plenty of money to get us through our RTW 3.0 to Northern Asia (China, Japan, Korea, Taiwan, maybe Myanmar), though in reality, we were planning to spend the money we made in Thailand and save our honeyfund money for later in life, when we inevitably would return to the U.S. at some point. But the point is, instead of registering for material, often superfluous things like dishes, pots and pans, etc., we essentially registered for one year of traveling (which because we broke it up with teaching, actually equated to more like 3-4 years' worth of traveling). Now I ask you, at the end of those 3-4 years, what will have proven more valuable, the depreciated household items that we could have registered for but in reality already had, or the memories/pictures we accumulated from seeing more in a few years than most people will see over the course of their life?

So there it is. Even if traveling is not your thing, I hope you've seen how you don't have to succumb to the typical American tradition of registering for useless (or at best superfluous) household items simply to appease your guests by not asking them directly for money. Instead, if you're not keen on simply asking for money, which personally I think is fine, use something like a honeyfund to register for things you actually need/want in life, not things you already have but could use slight upgrades of. I remember when my friend got married I perused through her registry and couldn't believe some of the things she was registering for. One thing that really struck me was a set of fine China (aka dishes) for several hundred dollars. When I asked her, "Don't you already have dishes?"

She replied, "Yes, but we want a set of really nice ones to use for special occasions."

All I could think at the time was she's registering for fine China, and I'm registering for a trip to China, literally.

Like the engagement ring and wedding, it's doubtful that many Americans will change their habits when it comes to wedding gift registries, for they're too stuck in their ways and frankly, too concerned with appearances (aka Keeping Up with the Joneses) to risk being seen as outliers. But I urge you, if/when you get married (or if you're already married, when your kids get married, assuming you have or will have them), think about these issues very carefully. While it's true a wedding only happens once (if you're lucky) in your life, the impact of it can last a lifetime. And while it's understandable that you want to impress and appease your family and friends by buying your future wife a huge diamond ring, throwing a lavish party, and requesting "essential" gifts that any young couple needs to start their lives together, think about the fact that when all of the dust settles, and everyone goes back to their daily, mundane lives, no longer thinking of the eternal bliss that is you and your wife, what will you be left with (other than hopefully each other)? The answer, for a typical American, is usually a mountain of debt and house full of unnecessary crap. Before being faced with that situation, consider whether there's a better alternative, even if it's a road less traveled.

Kids

The last component to marriage that people (not just Americans) typically take for granted and just assume is a way of life, is having kids. Now let's be clear here, I'm not telling you not to have kids. Not at all. But what I am saying, is that before doing so, realize that it will be the biggest financial, emotional and physical/time commitment you will ever make in life. And after you have one, every significant decision you make for the rest of your life (and most of the insignificant ones) will be based at least in part, if not entirely, on your kid(s).

What strikes me as most odd about this issue is the cavalier attitude and nonchalance with which people (again, not just Americans, but all people) choose to have kids. And not just one kid, but multiple kids. For a middle-class American family, it is estimated to cost approximately $241,000 to raise a child from birth to the age of eighteen.[27] And that doesn't include the cost of college nor the cost of any private education before the age of eighteen, nor does it include daycare or anyone watching after your kids in exchange for payment. Moreover, that doesn't include the tens (if not hundreds) of thousands of dollars you're likely to spend on your child after the age of eighteen, for big things

---

[27] http://money.cnn.com/2013/08/14/pf/cost-children/index.html.

like weddings, cars, or housing, or even just small things like meals, presents and vacation. If the average middle-class American saves $10,000 a year, that means they'll need to work twenty-four more years just to support one kid. Forty-eight more years (or more likely, a higher-paying job or much lower standard of living) to support two. Yet, people make the decision to have kids every day without thinking twice, largely because they think that's what's expected of them.

A few examples illustrate my point of how the world has come to accept having kids almost as a formality, something that every married couple should do, regardless of circumstance. The first example is the reaction my ex and I received when we told people we were quitting our high-paying (but high hours and high stress) corporate jobs to travel the world and move to Asia. Though those that knew and loved us most knew it was a very planned, calculated, careful decision, and one that would almost surely work out great for us, for those that didn't know us well, the general reaction was "Wow. That's crazy."

In reality, however, our decision was a one-year commitment, which we eventually turned into four. But if we didn't like living in Thailand, we could always move somewhere else, or just come home. While it's true we likely couldn't have gone back to the same jobs we had before we left (though my ex likely could have since she worked with her brother, and I left on good terms with my firm so I might have been able to as well), we didn't like our jobs to begin with, so we likely would have quit them even if we weren't taking the trip of ten thousand lifetimes. So at worst, our trip was a one-year commitment (though in reality we could have come home at any time, even if only after a few days).

Now contrast this with having kids, which is a minimum eighteen-year financial and legal commitment, but really a lifelong commitment. Whenever you hear that someone is having a baby, the reaction is always the same: Wow, that's amazing, congrats, mazel tov, etc. No one ever says "Wow, that's crazy!!!". But my question is, why? Why is it crazy to quit a job you don't like to travel the world with your new wife, knowing that you can come back home anytime you want, but it's not crazy to commit to being a parent for the rest of your life, when in reality, you have no idea about what parenthood entails? If for some reason you don't like it (or worse, can't afford it), you can't return your kid. You can give it up for adoption of course, but that comes with a whole host of other ethical, moral and financial considerations. So why then, do people think it's crazy to make a one-year commitment but no one ever questions the merit of making a lifelong commitment?

A second example of the nonchalance with which the world has come to accept having children occurred all of the time when my ex and I were traveling. Whenever anyone heard our story, particularly older people, the reaction was always the same: "Wow, that's amazing. Do you guys have kids?" When we said no, the answer was always either "Why not?" or "Just wait until you do." Let's look closely at both of these responses. The first one, "Why not?" It's hard to believe that we live in a society where if you're married and don't have kids, something seems wrong with you.[28] Knowing everything we know that's entailed with having children (nine months of excruciating labor, a lifetime of financial commitment, sleep deprivation, likely a loss of sex, intimacy, health, exercise, alone time, etc.), shouldn't the question be why do you want to have kids, instead of why don't you?

I'm not saying there aren't good reasons to have kids (and frankly, my ex and I were still undecided at the time I began

---

[28] Of course, nowadays, people are having fewer children, or in many instances, no children at all.
https://www.nytimes.com/2018/07/05/upshot/americans-are-having-fewer-babies-they-told-us-why.html.

writing this book and she subsequently had one with her new husband and now has three, the latter two twins), but it amazes me that the default in our society is to ask someone why they don't want to have children, rather than why they want them. Looking at it from a purely economic standpoint, as consumers, we question each and every purchase we make, from a $5 latte at Starbucks to a new luxury automobile, but we don't question the biggest financial commitment we'll ever make, having kids. And even more amazing, people don't just stop at one kid, but they have multiple, often at the expense of their retirement, lifestyle, or even their kids' well-being. So I urge you, before having children, ask yourself why you really want them. And the next time you hear someone tell you they're pregnant, try asking them why? Though this obviously won't sit well with them, query whether it's any more inappropriate than asking a married couple why they don't have kids.

Going back to my 2nd example above, the second reaction we often received when telling people we don't have kids was, "Just wait until you do." No one ever said "Well, if you do, you won't be able to travel like you do." Or no one ever asked if we wanted them. Instead, they said *when* you do, as if it's a given. Again, when did our society become such that it was just expected for married people to have kids, as if it's some sort of absolute. Per above, statistically, married couples nowadays are having fewer kids, and many young married couples in particular are choosing not to have any kids at all.[29] Yet, on the whole, our society (both Americans and non-Americans) still expects married people to have kids

---

[29] *Id.* Presumably lack of money or not willing to work into your elderly years is the primary reason young people are choosing to have fewer children or no children at all, but even Seth Rogen and his wife have repeatedly said they don't have children because they love their life and wouldn't be able to do the same things they currently do if they had children.

(if nothing else for the continued existence of the human race and their respective countries), so much so that they just assume you will, and if you don't, they think something is wrong you. Now *that* is what I call crazy.

On a related note, for those of you that do already have kids and therefore think it's impossible for you to travel like my wife and I have traveled, or impossible for you to take a similar risk, we saw plenty of people working/living overseas with their children during our travels. In fact, on our very first flight from Seattle to Lima, Peru when we first left the U.S., we met a young couple traveling with their two kids. Like us, they too were teachers, and they had just finished teaching in Indonesia for a couple of years. At the time they were next on their way to Peru to teach there, with a short layover in the U.S. to catch up with family and friends. Another couple we met while living in Asia was sailing across the world with a kid in tow (talk about a great/cultural upbringing!!). And the woman I'm now dating is currently contemplating moving to the Caribbean with her kids so she can rediscover her love of sailing (she's skipper certified) and to show them there's more to life than the same tiny corner of the world where they've lived to date. So contrary to popular belief, it is possible to pursue your personal and professional dreams even after you have children. And while your personal happiness will surely increase, dare I argue that your kids will be far better off for it as well.

The third example of the often taken for granted significance of having kids comes from my own personal life. As I discussed earlier in this book, my father was a man who often lived beyond his means. He enjoyed the finer things in life, and often struggled to keep up financially. He and my mom got divorced when I was three (and my older sister was six), and for as long as I can remember, my mom struggled to receive child support from him. Shortly after the divorce from my mom, he married again, and had two more kids. His move to LA really crippled him financially, as he could never keep up with the lavish LA lifestyle he sought so hard to live. One day, I vividly recall him saying to me, "Do you know how rich I'd be if I never had kids?"

Now granted this is something you should never tell your child if you do in fact have one, even if you feel this way, but I will never forget those words. While he wasn't saying he regretted having kids, he was saying that all of his financial problems would be non-existent if he hadn't had kids. And this was a man who at the end of his life was making approximately $500,000 a year. However, it wasn't enough to support his four kids. Yet, every day, in America and elsewhere, people have kids while making far less money. Typically, it entails huge financial sacrifices on the part of the parents (e.g., moving from the city to the suburbs, less or even no vacation, working two or more jobs that you don't enjoy, etc.). For the lucky ones, hopefully their lifestyle is such that they still enjoy the basic necessities of life (e.g., a nice home, maybe a car, clothing, food, maybe some entertainment once in a while and if they're really "lucky" a one or two week vacation every year). Sadly, for many others however, having children not only results in the loss of their own financial freedom, but the loss of their kids' as well.[30]

Having lived in Bangkok, Thailand and traveled through most of Southeast Asia (as well as South America and parts of Africa), I have seen more poverty than I care to imagine. Throughout all of it, what saddens me the most is seeing children in poverty. With rare exception, a child born into poverty will die in poverty, for their opportunities for success are few and far between. It absolutely fathoms me to see

---

[30] In fact, in a recent UK study, 1 in 12 parents (or 8.3%) regretted having kids. That's a pretty staggering number for something that's almost universally celebrated with "congrats," "mazel tov," etc., instead of the more appropriate "are you sure this is what you really want and also can you really afford it?" https://yougov.co.uk/topics/education/articles-reports/2021/06/24/one-twelve-parents-say-they-regret-having-children.

mothers begging for money while holding their infant children (or equally abundant, sending their children up to strangers to beg for money, or as I experienced in South America, sending their children to pickpocket tourists). I often wonder what in the world made them choose to have that child, when they clearly couldn't even afford to take care of themselves.

For many of them, their choice to have a child (or often another) is often the result of a government policy which provides welfare to people with children. So the more children you have, the more welfare you receive. To me, this seems like a counterproductive solution. As I mentioned, a child born into welfare is almost guaranteed to die on it. To me, nothing would be worse than being born into poverty/welfare. So why then, do governments continue to encourage bringing children into poverty by offering subsidies for bearing more children? If anything, I would think government policy should be the opposite (i.e., if you're on welfare and have another child, you will be cut-off from welfare). This would discourage bringing children into poverty, a noteworthy goal, I believe.

For better or worse, there's no test for being a parent. In other words, health abiding, anyone can have a child. It's pretty remarkable if you think about it. You need a license to drive, a license to drink, a license to vote, a license to marry, a license to carry a firearm, but you don't need a license to be a parent. Think how much better off our world might be if you had to take a test every time you wanted to have a kid. Surely, this wouldn't affect the majority of people who have children and have the financial and emotional capacity to care for them. But it would prevent people who can't afford to have children (let alone even take care of themselves) from having children. Personally, I would rather not be born than be born into poverty.

An example of this is when I would teach my students about the issue of gay marriage. Being a teacher in Thailand, when I discussed the issue of gay marriage as a means of introducing the concept of a debate, not surprisingly, approximately half of my Thai students were against it (Thailand is a traditionally conservative country, though surprisingly it has a very prevalent gay population). One of the common reasons they asserted against gay marriage is because every child should be born with a mom and a dad, not two dads or two moms. In response, I typically posed the following question: if they had to choose between being born into poverty but with a mom and a dad, versus being adopted by two moms or two dads who were financially stable and would be able to provide for them and give them all of life's necessities, which would they choose. Of course, inevitably, they all say the two moms or two dads, particularly because I taught at a very affluent university where a number of my students drove luxury automobiles to school and were only going to college (which their parents were paying for) so they could take over their parents' business.

The point is, when gay couples want to adopt, unlike every other parent who just needs a working penis or vagina, and a willing partner, gay parents (or any parent looking to adopt) do need to take a test. They need to apply for adoption, which involves a lengthy screening process whereby the adoption agency makes sure you have the means and foundation to care for the child. They inspect your home, your family, your relationships, your past, and most importantly, your finances. Only if they deem you fit to be a parent will you be eligible for adoption. Why, I query, is this process only for parents seeking adoption? Wouldn't our world be far better off if everyone had to take a screening test in order to have a child (or at least to qualify for certain government subsidies which frankly and sadly is precisely the reason why so many people do have kids)? It would certainly prevent parents bringing children into a world of poverty, which I would argue, is essentially the same as killing them.

Taking into account all of the above, I ask you again, when did our society become such that people just expect you to have children, and if you don't, something is wrong with you? As I said before, I'm not saying having children is a bad idea, and as I said, my ex-wife and I at the time of this writing were still undecided as to whether we wanted children (she clearly made a definitive decision), but make no mistake about it, having children is the biggest commitment a person can ever make in their life (far more significant than getting married, buying a house or car, or taking or quitting a job). All of those are temporary decisions: if you don't like the outcome, you can change it. Such is not the case with children. So many things can change over time (e.g., your marriage, your financial situation, your health, etc.), yet people choose to have children every day, often without thinking twice. And all of this assumes your child will be born healthy. God forbid he/she is born with some sort of defect, or similarly perhaps you were financially prepared (barely) for one child but then end up having twins, or even triplets. Unlike a spouse, house, car, or even job, you can't return a child (adoption aside). So before having one (or two/three), you better be 100% sure that you want them, and that you can afford to take care of them for the rest of your life, regardless of circumstance. Even if it means downsizing your lifestyle and working more hours for more years at a job you don't like, or perhaps even hate. And if you do decide to have a child, make sure your marriage is rock solid, because take it from personal experience, nothing is worse than getting a divorce when kids are involved.

So the next time you hear someone say they're having a kid, instead of saying congrats, ask them why. And when they look at you like you're crazy, tell them certainly they must have good reasons for making a lifetime financial, emotional, and physical commitment. And if they don't, then maybe you should tell them they're crazy.

140

As an aside, one of the many things I've found to be remarkable about living in Colorado, where I've been for the past several years (more below on how that came to be), is that women on dating apps which I've recently been forced to use go out of their way to explicitly state they don't want children. The remarkable part is they don't even have to answer the question, but they want their potential future partner to know that kids are not in the cards for them. And many of these women are in their 20s and 30s, presumably fully capable of giving birth. But Colorado, with all its outdoor activities and general increased quality of life as compared to most other American places, tends to attract women (and men) who simply have other, more important priorities in life than having children. And frankly, that's one of the many reasons I love it and consider it to be one of the best places in America to live. Simply put, my married friends with kids often spend their weekends watching (or in rare instances, "coaching") their kids play sports. Coloradoans, however, myself included, prefer to play and actively participate in sports (e.g., skiing, hiking, rock climbing, mountain biking, paddle boarding/kayaking/ canoeing, etc.).

Cost of Living and Commuting

The last piece to the puzzle of abandoning the traditional American way of living (corporate job, 50 hours/week, 50 weeks/year) is evaluating your cost of living situation. Although touched upon in earlier sections, it's such an important piece that it merits its own section.

As described earlier, I spent the first five years of my professional life in Chicago and the following three in NYC. Both of those cities are two of the most expensive cities to live in the U.S., and the latter arguably the most expensive. To live comfortably, you need to make at least $100,000/year. Fortunately, I made almost twice that so I was able to both live comfortably, and save considerably (approximately $5,000/month).

However, when my ex and I moved to Thailand, my salary was 10% of what I made in the U.S. Fortunately, however, we received free housing, so the biggest expense for most people was no expense for us. But even without the free housing, you can find decent housing in Bangkok for approximately $300-500/month (in 2013, at least). By way of comparison, in NYC, a city of equal size (approximately 8 million people), we were paying approximately $3,000/month in rent. So even though my salary was approximately 10% of what I made in the U.S., our cost of living was also approximately 10%, which meant our standard of living didn't really change at all.

This is an important consideration for anyone when deciding where to live. Just because a job pays more doesn't mean you'll make or save more. For example, before deciding to quit our jobs and travel/move to Thailand, I was considering an in-house legal opportunity in a small town in Pennsylvania. The pay was approximately $125,000/year, a substantial decrease from my Chicago/NY salaries of approximately $200,000/year. But if we moved to a small town in PA, our cost of living would substantially reduce, so I likely would have saved about the same amount. Ultimately I decided not to pursue that opportunity (namely because I couldn't stomach the idea of living in a small town), but the point is, I would never have considered a job in Chicago or NYC for $125,000/year, but in rural PA, I considered it.

Similarly, nothing frustrates me more than when people think my ex and I lived in a third-world/developing country. While Thailand may have certain third-world/developing aspects to it, Bangkok, where we lived, is a first-world city. In fact, in some respects, it's far more first-world than Chicago and NYC, and certainly more first-world than many rural places in America. For example, as described above, at our school, a private university in Bangkok, our students often drove luxury automobiles to/from class, and some even took taxis. Similarly, they all had the latest smartphones, far better than ours. And while most of the time we ate cheap local Thai food (namely because it was delicious), at least once or twice a week we'd go out for a nice "Western" meal (e.g., Italian, burgers, Mexican, etc.) at a trendy restaurant in Bangkok, but for a fraction of what we would pay in the States. Finally, as another example, almost every weekend we would see a new Hollywood movie (the same movies being shown in the U.S., usually before they even came out in the U.S.) but again, for about 1/3 of the price, in nicer/fancier theaters. In fact, we even saw our first Hollywood movie in 4D. By comparison, at the time, there was only one 4D theater in the U.S. which showed feature length Hollywood films, and it was in L.A. The point is, although I made approximately 5% of what I made in the U.S., my standard of living remained the same in Thailand. The only difference is I actually had the time to enjoy it.

Another important factor in the cost of living component is state and city taxes. When I lived in Chicago, I paid approximately 3% in state tax, but little or no city tax. When we moved to NYC, however, I paid a 3-4% state tax, and also a 3% city tax. An additional 3-4% may not seem like a lot, but when you make $200,000/year, that's $6,000-7,000. In fact, we were so annoyed by the NYC tax that we almost considered moving to Hoboken, New Jersey, which is right across the river from NYC, but it would have increased my daily commute by about thirty minutes each way, which as discussed below, wouldn't have been palatable for me (if I had worked on the West side of Manhattan, however, instead of the East side, my commute time likely wouldn't have changed). If I ever move back to NYC, however, I may very well try to live somewhere like Hoboken so as to avoid that city tax. Likewise, that's also one of the reasons I decided to get licensed to practice law in Texas before we left the States. Texas, like Florida (though in Florida they require you to take the bar exam) has no state tax. This is just another factor to consider when calculating your cost of living. And not surprisingly, it's also one of the many reasons people have been fleeing states like California, New York and Illinois in recent years, all with high taxes and high everything,[31] for states like Texas and Florida.

Equally as important as the cost of living and also often overlooked, is the commuting factor. For my entire life, I have always been able to walk to my school or work and I have never had more than a 15-20-minute commute. As proclaimed at the outset of this book, for me, nothing is more valuable than my time, and so personally, I could never commute an hour (or likely even 30 minutes) to/from work every day. I would much rather spend that time working out, with my family, or doing something else productive. I have never been able to understand people who live in the suburbs and

---

[31] It always amazes me when I drive between my homes in Denver and Myrtle Beach how the cost of things like gas, cigarettes and even marijuana remarkably increase as you go from "red" states to "blue" states. For example, a pack of cigarettes (which I'll buy on rare occasion) costs approximately $10 in Denver, $15 in Chicago and $5 in South Carolina. Literally the exact same pack/brand. Same goes for the cost of gas. And with marijuana, I can get 5-7 times the amount (literally) for the same price in Colorado as I can in Illinois, and frankly it's better quality. Equally unbelievable is how I don't pay a single highway toll from Colorado to Iowa but then the moment I hit Illinois I pay a toll every few miles it seems. Why??? If Illinois were a great state with great highways, public transportation, infrastructure, police protection, etc., I could see why. But it's not. In fact, more people have fled Illinois, per capita, over the last decade than any state other than West Virginia (generally regarded as the worst state in the U.S.). https://patch.com/illinois/chicago/more-people-left-illinois-any-other-state-last-year-study. How their (obese) governor gets away with charging some of the highest taxes in the country (on everything) when their state is riddled with crime and poor infrastructure is beyond me. But at least they still have the Chicago Bears (for now; there's been talk of even them fleeing the city for greener/presumably cheaper pastures in the suburbs of Arlington Heights).

commute an hour each way to work every single day. To me, that's crazy. But millions of Americans do it every day, so to each their own.

In fact, one of the reasons that my ex and I had such a great situation in Bangkok is because of our commuting situation. Our school was actually located about forty-five minutes outside of Bangkok (thirty minutes on a good day but ninety minutes if traffic was bad). However, they also had a city campus (which we didn't teach at, except when I taught at their law school for a few semesters), and our school provided free transportation between the two campuses. Because each teacher got one free accommodation (either at the suburban campus where we taught, or in the city), this meant that most teachers needed to decide whether they wanted to live on campus (basically in the middle of nowhere, and without a car, it was almost impossible to get around), or whether they wanted to commute approximately two hours every day.

Because my ex and I were both teachers, however, that meant we each got a free accommodation. Consequently, we chose to take one room at the suburban campus where we taught, and one room in the city. As a result, we typically spent four nights a week on campus (Mon-Thurs) and three nights (Fri-Sun) in the city. Thus, we only had to commute twice a week, instead of twice a day. Frankly, were it not for that amazing setup, I don't think we would have been able to teach at our school, as we often said we have no idea which of the two evils we'd have chosen if we could only have one free accommodation. There were several other teacher couples at our school but surprisingly we're the only ones who chose that setup. Some chose to take two rooms on campus and some chose to take two rooms in the city, but we were the only ones who asked to take a room at each (why I know not).[32]

In addition to saving us approximately two hours each day, we actually really enjoyed our setup. It's like we had two homes, our suburban home where we stayed during the week, and our city home where we stayed on the weekends. Every Friday, we got very excited to go back to the city for the weekend. But similarly, we were also happy to go back to the burbs (where it's much quieter and more peaceful than the often hectic Bangkok) on Monday mornings. It was really the perfect setup for us. Our suburban campus/home, like any good university, also had state of the art recreational facilities (basketball courts, Olympic-sized swimming pool, gym, tennis courts, etc.), so we were able to stay very fit/active during the week.

So the point is, money is just one factor when deciding what to do for a living and where to live. And although I've advocated saving as much money as possible and not spending money on frivolous things, sometimes, it may be worth taking a job for less money or spending a little more on rent (the latter solely to reduce your daily commute or to live in a particular neighborhood, not just so you can have extra space to store your superfluous, unnecessary material possessions), just to improve your quality of life.

Of course, the one caveat to this is that much has changed since the onset of the Covid-19 pandemic, and thus conceivably the concept of remote working and the notion of a daily commute might be forever changed too. With that said, certain industries (e.g., investment banking) might

---

[32] Even more remarkable, some teachers forewent the free housing all together and decided to find (and pay for) their own accommodation. Considering our school's free housing plan is a "use it or lose it" plan (i.e., if you don't use it, you don't get any extra compensation), why anyone wouldn't take the free housing, even if they wanted separate, additional housing, is beyond me.

always want their employees to work in the office. For as the CEO of Morgan Stanley, James Gorman, recently said, "If you want to get paid New York rates, you work in New York. None of this, I'm in Colorado and work in New York and am getting paid like I'm sitting in New York City. Sorry, that doesn't work."

Damn I do love living in Colorado!!!!

Part Seven
Final Thoughts

Of the many life lessons I've learned while traveling and living abroad, perhaps the one that stood out the most is that it was often the people who have the least amount of tangible possessions who seemed to enjoy life the most.

I've struggled mightily trying to come up with an ending for this book because the truth is, I initially began writing this book during my travels abroad, when I was still married, and before returning to the U.S. While I certainly have some new/different perspectives since moving back to the U.S. in July 2016, the core of what I've written herein remains intact. With that said, here are a few of the main principles I'd like to end with, as well as a personal note about the life I've carved out for myself in America and why it unfortunately didn't work out with the, at one time, love of my life.

First, no matter how it pans out, I know I will never regret for even a second taking the leap of faith my ex and I took in June 2013. Although I may never achieve the level of financial success I might have been able to obtain had I stuck around big law and made partner in my late 30s/early 40s, I also know that, generally speaking, I did not enjoy my job, and consequently most days, I dreaded the thought of going to work. On top of that, I worked 60-70 hours/week with only two weeks of vacation a year. Sure, I made a lot of money, but I was never able to spend it. I suppose I could have spent it on materialistic, ego-satisfying possessions like designer clothes, fancy cars, superfluous household items, extravagant vacations twice a year, etc., but as explained earlier, that's just not my style. So instead, I saved until I felt comfortable enough to take this journey.

So even if I'm never able to make as much money as I once earned, I know I would have quit my job at some point simply because I didn't enjoy it. And as a teacher in Thailand, not only did I actually enjoy my job, but I only worked 15-20 hours/week, and I got four months of vacation per year. But perhaps most satisfying, I got to spend more time with my ex in a few years than most married couples will spend in twenty years, and we got to do the things we most enjoyed doing in life, together (e.g., traveling, working out, watching movies, cooking, eating out, etc.). Granted, spending that much time together is one of the several reasons we likely weren't able to stay together, but nonetheless, I wouldn't trade that time we spent together for anything.

Second, I will never take a job again just for the money. For one, to be frank, as a result of my hard work and dedication early in life, and also my relatively frugal lifestyle, I simply don't need it. The fact of the matter is that I've made more money off my investments in the past several years, particularly with Covid-19 and the unique combination of a) having extra time on my hands to spend researching investments and b) arguably the only time in the stock market's history where you could "time the market" if you researched correctly and bought into the "correct" stocks (e.g., the stay-at-home stocks). But had I been working 50+ hours/week, 50 weeks/year like at my previous lawyer jobs, I wouldn't have had the time to do the required research. In other words, I've learned in the past several years that I (and many others if you have the discipline, fortitude and foresight) can make more money by spending time *wisely* investing the money I've already made, than simply continuing to accumulate more money via the traditional rat race way. Ideally, some combination of both is the way to go.

Alternatively, and not completely out of the realm of possibility, I could retire in Thailand right now and never work another day in my life (though the visa issue might prove difficult, at least until I turn 50). More realistically, I'll likely continue living in the U.S. for the next several years, expanding upon my already solid real estate portfolio, and if really needed which hopefully shouldn't be the case, I can always go back to doing independent contractor work for major law firms/companies like I was doing when I originally returned to the U.S. in 2017, which generally speaking, allowed me to work about 50% of the hours I used to work, for 50% of the pay. And while I'm hoping to find love (and a life partner again), if all else fails, I'll likely return to Thailand at the age of 50 when I can get a retirement visa and live "happily ever after."

As for my burgeoning real estate portfolio, as you likely know, Airbnb changed the game of real estate. Prior to its existence, real estate investment meant you buy a property, somebody pays your mortgage, and then in 30 years you own that property free and clear and presumably it's gone up in value. But if you decide (or need) to sell in less than 30 years, particularly less than five, there's a chance the value of your property may have gone down.

Airbnb, on the other hand, involves all of the above same principles but also includes generating significant cash flow on a yearly basis. A good Airbnb can generate a 20-25% annual return, meaning if you put $100,000 down on a $400,000 condo/house, after paying your mortgage and all expenses, you can still generate $20,000-25,000 on that property. And a great Airbnb, like the one I own in Denver, can generate double that amount while also allowing you to live there 3-6 months a year. Suffice to say, Airbnb is an absolute game changer for real estate investment, and I intend to continue taking full advantage of it.

But under no circumstance will I ever go back to working 50 hours/week, 50 weeks/year, for someone else, doing something I don't particularly enjoy. Life is too short, and if my time abroad taught me anything, it's that you really don't need that much money to live comfortably. For example, when I lived in Bangkok, I made $1,000/month which allowed me to live comfortably eight months out of the year, and travel the remaining four, all while still saving a little money. Moreover, Americans are the only developed country in the world (outside of maybe Japan) where people spend the vast majority of their "prime years" working relentlessly to *hopefully* enjoy the last 20 years of their life, assuming they live that long. Even if they do live that long, however, they'll be 60-80 years old and inevitably unable to do the things they could have done when they were younger. For example, climbing mountains, skiing black or double black diamonds, scuba diving, etc. Or even if they can still do them, they certainly won't be able to do them to the extent they could have when they were younger.

A simple story from a trip I recently took to Alabama to golf the world-renowned Robert Trent Jones golf trail (26 courses throughout the State built by arguably golf's greatest course architect) illustrates this point. At one of the courses, the group behind me consisted of three elderly gentlemen. These men, while seemingly "fit" and healthy, were likely in their 80s or maybe even 90s. Consequently, they were playing from the ladies' tees and catching up to me on every hole (I was actually playing solo just ahead of them, but playing from tees much further back). All I could think about each time they caught up to me was "I hope these guys didn't work relentlessly their entire adult life just so they can tee off from the ladies' tees at the age of 80 or 90, as that would be really sad." Instead, wouldn't it be much better to play more golf (or pursue whatever your passion is) when you're younger and can hit the ball a lot further, even if it means having to work a little more when you're older. Personally, I'd make that trade-off every single time. But Americans are literally the only developed country in the world (besides Japan in my personal experience) that routinely don't. And even worse, God forbid you do something like me and my ex-wife did, quitting our jobs at the age of 33 and 26 respectively to travel the world for four years, and everyone will call you "crazy."

To me, the much crazier thing is working relentlessly during the prime of your life all to *hopefully* enjoy the last 20 years of your life. As suggested, even if you're fortunate enough to be alive and "healthy," you certainly won't be able to do the things you could do in your twenties, thirties or forties, or at least not to the extent you could do them then. So instead, I suggest you try to "flip the script" and take some time off in your earlier years to accomplish some more personal goals or even just to travel/adventure more, and if you have to work a little more in your later years, so be it. For the typical corporate American who just sits at their desk most of the day anyways, I'd much prefer to do that when I'm older and can't move around as well to begin with, rather than when I'm younger in the prime of my life. But hey, that's just me, and every other developed country in the world besides the United States and Japan.

The third and final thing I learned with certainty from my travels is that, no matter how difficult life may seem at times, always remember, someone (and in fact millions if not billions of people) have it rougher than you. And what's most remarkable is that it's often the people who have less who seem to enjoy life the most. Funny how that works, but time and time again I've found it to be true. Whether in Thailand, South America, India, Nepal or anywhere else in SE Asia, the less people have, the happier (and more generous) they seem to be. For example, when I lived in Bangkok, there was a group of homeless people who lived down the block from me and my ex. We would often pass them when we were out for a run or heading to/from dinner. They always smiled at us, and sometimes they even offered us some of their beer (to which we always politely declined, of course). And on several occasions, they even asked *us* how *we* were doing (as opposed to the majority of homeless people in America who often ask for money). To reiterate, they were homeless, and they asked US how WE were doing. Imagine that. All I could think about was that no matter how bad of a day I could have been having (and in Thailand, bad days are few and far between), it could never be as bad as their best day, for after all, they're homeless.

But that's just one of many examples of the people I've met (or observed) along my travels who helped shape the way I think about life. An equally invaluable lesson I've learned in life after all of my travels is that I will never need or want for anything in life again. During my four plus years traveling the world, I slept in the jungle on mats with nothing to protect me from the mosquitoes or other jungle creatures other than a mosquito net, slept in wooden huts in local villages miles from civilization, caught my own food, went days and even weeks without showering, took countless cold showers and slept in countless non-air conditioned rooms with only a fan to protect me from the Asia heat, peed and pooped in places you can't even imagine, took countless buses, trains, ferries, motorcycle taxis, jeepneys, rickshaws and every other conceivable form of public and private transportation you can imagine, ate snake, dog, squirrel, and many other foods that most first-world countries would only consider as pets, and had countless other experiences that most people only read about in books (e.g., I've been robbed in at least a half dozen countries including by the police on several occasions, but I'm still here). And for me, those were once in a lifetime experiences, but for the locals who so kindly provided us with the opportunity to share those experiences (not the robberies) with them, they were everyday experiences.

As a result, I will never again complain when the internet or cable goes out (unless it's during a Chicago Bears; everyone has their breaking point:), I will never complain about having to take a cold shower, sleep in a hot room, take public transportation, go to the bathroom in a less than ideal

153

location, or eat something that others may consider inedible. For all of these things are things that Americans take for granted on an everyday basis, whereas for the majority of the rest of the world, they are luxuries. This, above all, is what I learned from my travels. That is, you don't need much to enjoy life. Really, you just need your health, your time, and the freedom to enjoy it with the people you love most. If you have those three things, then you just need a minimal amount of money for food, shelter, clothing and perhaps some entertainment. Everything else is superfluous. But without time, all the money in the world won't help you. For as the saying goes, you can't take your money with you to the grave.

Brief Addendum

For those who are curious why it did not ultimately work out with me and my now ex-wife, there were several significant reasons, but the crux of it was we both wanted different things upon our return, an issue I tried to raise with her and her parents when, as you might recall, they initially requested we get married before, rather than after, our travels. Without going into too much detail, my ex, who is seven years younger than me, upon our return to the U.S., started a family business in Columbus, OH where she is from. We moved there in July 2016 and I stayed for two years (after we initially agreed to only one), but really I knew after two weeks that Columbus, OH was not where I would be spending the rest of my life, and where she likely will. For one, I wasn't licensed to be a lawyer there and thus would have had to take the Ohio bar or wait five years to waive into the bar like I did with New York, Colorado, Texas and Washington, prior to leaving the U.S. For two, it rains approximately 170 days/year in Ohio, a fact I was completely unaware of until moving there in July and experiencing rain for two straight weeks.

Ultimately, for a kid from Chicago who had spent the majority of his life, sans college and law school, in Chicago, New York and Bangkok, Ohio was just too small/rural for me and also after two straight weeks of rain I immediately realized why I had sworn off the Midwest as a potential landing spot upon our return to the U.S., prior to leaving in 2013. In fact, I don't believe in God but I do believe in signs and two of them came to me while I was living in Columbus which confirmed that was not the place for me. First, it rained so much one day that our entire closet flooded, but only my side. My ex -wife's clothes were untouched; mine were ruined. Second, after spending months unsuccessfully applying to teaching jobs at universities and law schools in the U.S., I had a Skype (Zoom still wasn't a thing then) call with Baylor University for a law school teaching position. The day of the call, it rained so much in Columbus that our internet went out, and I had to take the call from a coffee shop across the street. Needless to say, the call was a complete disaster and that's when I knew it was time to go back to my original plan of moving to Colorado upon my return to the U.S., where my ex-wife literally filled out my bar application prior to leaving the U.S., along with Texas and Washington state. Ohio was never even discussed, but as I said, people change and so I can't blame her for wanting to stay close to her family after being away for so many years.

So fast forward eight years later (to 2024), and I'm still in Colorado, still practicing law occasionally but more real estate of late and always on my terms now (e.g., I like to work approx. 20 hrs/week and take 3-4 months off a year, or take contract jobs that last several weeks or months at a time, allowing me equally long breaks in between to pursue my personal passions or real estate endeavors/other businesses/investments), even if it means making 50% of what I used to make (in exchange for getting the other 50% of my life/time back). For as outlined in this book, I've taken the steps in life to afford myself that flexibility and not be forced into working 50 hours/week, 50 weeks/year at a job I've never particularly loved. I'd rather spend that extra 50% of my time, including taking the aforementioned 3-4 months of vacation a year, doing the things I really enjoy doing (e.g., skiing, golfing, hiking, working out, spending time with friends and family), even if it means sacrificing a little in terms of material things discussed above like the size of my home, the type of watch I wear, etc. My ex-wife on the other hand, is remarried to a man from Ohio, bought a house in the suburbs near her parents and just had her third kid in the last two years (the 2nd two were twins). That was never going to be my life, but I'm happy she found hers.

For anyone who's curious why I chose Colorado to live, it's precisely the same reason I would never have a long commute to work, and also why I would never marry/be partners with someone who didn't enjoy the same activities as me, or is a vegetarian/vegan. Point being, Colorado has all of the outdoor activities I enjoy in life (skiing, hiking, mountain biking, golf, rafting/kayaking/tubing/paddleboarding), and best/most important of all, a world-class city (Denver) to base myself. Compared to a city like Chicago for example, which in and of itself is a world-class city (putting aside its 6 months of winter, high taxes, corrupt politicians and the fact that it's the homicide capital of the developed world), but it's greatest downfall and reason I can likely never live there again, is there's nothing world-class around Chicago. In other words, whenever you have that precious free time I alluded to earlier in the book, if you live in a city like Chicago, you need to get on a plane to go anywhere else world-class. Whereas in cities like New York, Los Angeles, San Francisco, San Diego, and Denver, all world-class cities though each flawed in their own way, you have access to world-class activities within a 1-2 hour drive of the city. And with my mantra in life being nothing is more precious than your time, I can never again live anywhere where I can't easily access world-class activities that I thoroughly and routinely enjoy.[1]

In fact, over the past several years, particularly since Covid when my lawyer hours dropped off significantly as a lot of my work was travel-dependent and I consequently began investing in real estate which has increased my passive cash flow and allowed me to work less, I've had numerous opportunities to go back into the practice of law, both full-time and even recently part-time. And each time the opportunity presented itself, I've passed (particularly full-

---

[1] As a practical matter, living in Denver, most weekends in the winter I go up to the mountains and stay the weekend (either at a hotel/Airbnb or one winter I had a "ski share" with a dozen or so other people). But in the rare instances where I'll just go for the day (1.5-3 hours each way depending on what time you leave/return), I'm always in awe when I return to Denver and realize I just skied a world-class resort during the day and then I'm back in a world-class city where I can go to a nice restaurant, catch a NBA/NHL/MLB/NFL game (all within walking distance of my condo), see a Broadway show, etc. in literally the same day. The reason why I originally chose Denver/Colorado to live upon my return to the U.S. (after my aforementioned brief stint in Ohio), is precisely because, growing up as a kid, my dad used to take me on ski trips to Colorado/out West once a year. And each time, he'd spend thousands of dollars, hope for good weather, inevitably not get it, and then as soon as we returned home we'd read about the snow dump that immediately followed. And each time, I'd say to myself, when I get older/am financially independent, I'm just going to move to Colorado so that I don't have to hope/pray for good weather the one week each year I spend thousands of dollars and take my 50% of vacation time. Instead, whenever it "dumps" in Colorado, even if it's a weekday, I can hit the slopes and get better skiing in a day than I would an entire year if I lived in a city like Chicago. Or similarly, if I have a work lull in the middle of the summer, I can hike a "14er" (aka 14,000-foot mountain) or go kayaking/paddle-boarding in the middle of the week. The few but not that rare instances that I've done this, are absolutely mind-blowing. And it's those times that I realize the importance of living within close proximity to the activities you most enjoy doing in life, whatever those activities may be. And newsflash, practicing law or sitting at a desk 50 hours/week, 50 weeks/year, is not chief among them, at least for me.

time) to continue the recent lifestyle I've carved out for myself (working approximately 20 hours/week, 30 weeks a year, whether it be on real estate, law or other investments/business endeavors I dabble in). For the truth is, contrary to what I might have suggested earlier in the book, when I was working 60+ hours/week, 50 weeks/year, almost entirely in an office,[2] I actually enjoyed being a lawyer in small doses or at times even regular doses. But the constant grind and never-ending billable hours were ultimately too much for me. And contrary to what that partner who went to Stanford undergrad and law school told me earlier in my career, I'm exceptionally good at it. Were I not, I wouldn't have lasted approximately fifteen years at three of the largest and most prestigious law firms in the world. But I also enjoy other things in life, such as golf, skiing, hiking, taking several vacations *a month* and several significant (2-4 weeks) vacations a year. And none of that would be possible if I returned to the typical 50 hour/week, 50 week/year American rat race lifestyle.

So I much prefer the life I have now, where although my hours/"salary"[3] might not be stable, whenever I hit a lull in work, I either enjoy my free time by engaging in any or all of the aforementioned Colorado (or more recently Myrtle Beach where my 2nd home/short-term rental is located) leisure

---

[2] Does anyone enjoy this lifestyle, other than perhaps Elon Musk? And if they tell you they do, I'm calling shenanigans.

[3] I say "salary" because, as discussed herein, most of my income these days comes from my variety of passive investments which I largely setup during Covid when my lawyer hours dropped off, the irony being I never would have had enough time to do the necessary research for those investments to be successful when I was still lawyering full-time. And it's also derived from the series of cognitive choices I made throughout the course of my life that most Americans simply don't have the discipline/foresight to make (i.e., foregoing large materialistic purchases and instead investing that money in stocks and ETFs/mutual funds, or more recently real estate that generates cash-flow).

activities, participating in a sports league (recall my friends are "coaching" them), exploring more real estate opportunities by literally driving across the U.S. (aka "driving for dollars"), or often just reading investment/business/self-help books to help further grow my financial portfolio and mental/physical well-being. Point being, I enjoy variety in my life, for as one of the many inspirational quotes I included above stated, "If you think adventure is dangerous, try routine. It is lethal."

Similarly, as another popular saying goes, in the end, it's the experiences we've had rather than the possessions we've accumulated that will ultimately make us happy and provide us with our fondest memories. And after reading this book, I'm hopeful that you too can live the life of your dreams, on your terms, by implementing some of the strategies and tactics advanced in this book. Even if this book impacts just a few people, my mission will have been accomplished. For life is too short to waste it away for years on end doing something you don't particularly enjoy doing, all so you can keep up with the Joneses. So carve out your own path in life, and if anyone questions it or calls you crazy, refer back to some of the lessons touted in here as well as some of the inspirational quotes which hopefully inspire you to create your own, successful and happy journey, however you choose to define those terms.

About the Author

Originally from Chicago and avid Bears fan, David Rosenfield is an accomplished commercial litigator who spent twenty years working for several AmLaw 100 law firms. Earlier in his career, he discovered sitting in an office chair was not the life he envisioned for himself and consequently made a plan to travel the world and move to Thailand with his American wife where they spent four years teaching English (and law for David) at a prestigious private university in Bangkok. After a lot of saving and hard work, David has traveled extensively throughout the world and visited 70 countries spanning six continents and 47 states in the U.S.A. Back in the U.S., David transitioned from law to real estate investor and now owns several properties that generate income for his current and future travels. His current goal is to travel to 100 countries (and the last 3 States) before the age of 50 and to retire in his favorite country, Thailand.

Printed in the USA
CPSIA information can be obtained
at www.ICGtesting.com
LVHW090743200924
791520LV00002B/287

9 798218 500481